Pepperoni Pizza

Poetry Anthology

Fall 2017

Pepperoni Pizza

Poetry Anthology

Shoestring Book Publishing, Maine, USA

**Published for
International Poetry Fellowship**

[Allpoetry.com - Kevin Watt, California, USA]

Pepperoni Pizza Poetry Anthology

Published for
International Poetry Fellowship

[Allpoetry.com - Kevin Watt, California, USA]

Paperback ISBN: 978-1-943974-11-5

Library of Congress Control Number: 2017951215

Layout and design by, Alison Wakefield & Allan Emery
Shoestring Book Publishing, Maine, USA

For information address;
shoestringpublishing4u@gmail.com
www.shoestringbookpublishing.com

IPF Founder: Ron Wiseman (AU)
IPF Chairman & Co-editor: Allan R. Emery (USA)
Treasurer & Co-editor: Alison Emery (USA)
IPF Anthology Publishing Group Moderator & Co-editor
Diane Gwynne Allen (USA)
Co-editor: James C. Allen

Dedication

To anyone who has ever Loved Poetry .....

Foreword

"Poetry is an echo, asking a shadow to dance." Carl Sandburg

If you were to ask anyone at AllPoetry how they ended up here with all of the other online poetry sites, you'd probably hear a different answer from each person. Thankfully we all found our way to AP and to this international anthology.

I have been with IPF for several years, and have helped edit since 2013. We all share a love for writing poetry and sharing our feelings of the art. In this anthology, like the others, you will find a wide range of poetry. Each anthology takes a theme.

Do you like pizza? Well the Pepperoni Pizza Anthology offers many toppings for you to enjoy: Cheesy, Moon dough pizza, thin crust, are a few tempting titles.

You'll also see rollicking poems of the moon, shadows, rivers and oceans.

Let this collection remind you that as humans, we live it all through a sense of fullness of time - joy, loss, play, thankfulness.

We are fortunate to be presented with a rich variety of voices moods and forms.

Now have a seat and a slice of pizza and work your way through this treasure.

Diane Gwynne Allen, Co-Editor

Winners of the International Poetry Fellowship Allpoetry contests

Gold Trophy Winners

Dave Kavanagh "A Wild Scudding Wind"
Norman Littleford (serious clown) "Counting My Blessings"
Michael Thomas "Achilles awakens"
Colleen Selvon-Rampersad (cosera) "cheesy" (haiku)
Satheesan Rangorth (Rangorth) "Moon Dough Pizza"
Michele Wass (Toomysterious) "One Sun Rises"

Silver Trophy Winners

Jack Mullen "Sounding Sea"
Michael Thomas "unselfish stories"
Ben Mosley (Benjamin Garrett) "To Live As Nature Has Designed"
Bobbie Jean Wright (Word Gatherer) "Old Soul"
Vivacious "mozzarella" haiku
Thomas Horton "Imitation"
Laurie F. Grommett (L.G.) "A Single Slice"

Bronze Trophy Winners

Don Skidmore (RoomKeys) "after life's latest storm"
Matthew Bower (Uneducated Poet) "Life's sweetest lessons"
William Rout "For Evermore"
Paul Geiger (Pauljg) "thin crust" haiku
Laurie F. Grommett (L.G.) "When In Rome …"
Thomas Burson (tomisb) "Turmoil"

Honorable Mention Trophy Winners

Bev Pollard (witterwax) "The Mermaid's Retreat"
Rupa Thomas (Stardust) "Small Expectations"
Alistair Muir (Al Muir) "Kogi Mam's Kin"
Diane Gwynne Allen (DianeAH) "Read Me"
Madhu Singh (tuni) "haiku"
Sue K. Green "The Ebb and Flow"

Dr. Asghar Nazeer "Isn't such love a gift of the Lord?"
Dayenoble "always more"
Sue K. Green "The Bluebird"
Kasi Senghor (Kasi) "without cheese"
Stephen W. Peake (StephenPk) "Bright Eyes"
Dave Kavanagh "Blackbird"
R.D. Stone (Rolinston) "Why Is A Heart Pulled Aside"
James Nichols (Mindful) "And Then I Die"
Maria Oday (Miz Rea) "A place to dwell"
Kasi Senghor (kasi) "Love Un-delayed"
Thomas N. Burson (tomisb) "The Last Note"
Rajkumar Mukherjee (rajkumar) "Ashawari"
Penelope Allen (PenAllen) "cheesy moon (haiku)"
Shades of Bill "Indian Summer"
David N. Betzer (David Betzer) "Tikkun"
Alf Collier "Neath Silvered Moon"
Cliff Lindemann (Cuul) "Mozzarella (haiku)"
James C. Allen "Mama Rosas, A Taste Of Italy"
Maria Oday (Miz Rea) "Ode to Cold Pizza"
Arianna Aleshire "Pizza"
Emilija Morkunaite (Emilija Mor)"the crust I knead"
Sue K. Green "Pizza"
HeartThrob "One Veggie Pizza Delight"
Sanjay Sudheendran (AquaHeart) "One"
Dave Kavanagh "Where the west wind goes"
Destiny Izehi (HuesFac3) "Spins"

Semi-Finalists

Katharine L. Sparrow (ksparrow) "Spellbound"
Essama Chiba (Esama Chiba) "Oceans Emotions"
Colleen Selvon-Rampersad (Cosera)"till you awake"
Melody Hamby Goss (Melody G) "The Mermaid"
Dave Hartford (Anguish) "Dance Of Dawn"
Laurie F. Grommett (L.G.)"Ocean Lessons"
Ann Gilchrist (Soulo) "She weeps in stars."
Kayanja Ronald Edwin (PoetR) "the midnight sail"
Debra M. Lalli (dml) "Floating"
grandniem "~~Ocean's Kiss~~ "

Joshua Joseph Bissot (Joshua joseph) "the shadow king"
Kiruthika Karthik (Sindhu selvi) "The Mahasagar
(In Hindi means, The Ocean)"
Iff Ur Abs "Peaceful Coexistence"
Cody Johnson (Gotha Tway) "Crescent Full Moon"
Bev Pollard (witterwax) "The Ballad of a Brave Man"
Chrissy Thompson (Chrissypoems) "Her"
Sandy Jo Botello (Inwalkedbud) "Full Circle"
Stephen Peake (StephenPK) "Measure of a Man"
Melody Hamby Goss (Melody G) "Earth Shadows"
Abhilaaj "Two Legged Mammals Molest
You Like Lamebrains"
Robert Szankowski (freeseeker) "A Name Already Known"
Destiny Izehi (HuesFac3)"Land of toys"
Dr. Asghar Nazeer "After the apocalypse has begun"
Laurie F. Grommett (L.G.) "Breaking Ground (Ottava Rima)"
-JR- "The Oracle"
Mark Moir "Society"
V.S. Paavolainen "Why on Earth"
Chrysanthy Pappas (Arria1) "Continuance"
RiAnne Hawley (LilacAura) "sliced tomatoes haiku"
James W. McRight Jr. (haikujourney)"Haiku #495 (thin crust)"
Donald G. Zielinski "mozzarella Bliss"
Mary Lou Healy (Mlou) "shocked cries"
Laurie F. Grommett (L.G.) "haiku (three toppings)"
Sam Irvin (ChaoticCosmos) "Cowabunga"
Firdous Arjumand "Save a couple of slices"
Tom Harmon (WholeHeart) "Not Bad"
Chris Daws (Chris the Rhymer) "Olives"
Brian Francis Kirkham (InkdropK) "Pizza"
Alf Collier "And Tomorrow Will Surely Come"

Table of contents

xiv

xvi

xix

xxviii

xxix

Preface on the

International Poetry Fellowship

from the beginning …

In early 2006, a poet and professor of English from Australia joined an online poetry group called AllPoetry. The day he signed on to write and share his poetry was a fortunate day indeed for hundreds of poets yearning to learn, to be recognized for their achievements, and to gather with poets of similar mind with a wish to succeed in the public venue. That man was Ron Wiseman. In the beginning, he also joined a small study group within AllPoetry called Inklings. It was modeled after a much smaller group of poets and writers from the United Kingdom that was led by the professor and author J.R.R. Tolkien in the early 20th century. That new Inklings group was led by Vera Rich (1936-2009), an internationally known poet and Belarusian translator from the UK, who had joined AllPoetry in the Fall of 2005. She insisted Ron take the authority to guide the group and to please her, he also added the W to the beginning of the group name. Hence: Winklings was born in 2006.

Winklings quickly became one of the premier writers' groups on AllPoetry. Members were selected by Ron based on a variety of qualities he desired to bring his family of poets into a class of their own. Dedication, talent, reputation, fortitude, a desire to succeed – all of these were qualities Ron sought when choosing his members. He would not be disappointed, either. Near the end of 2007, Winklings boasted about one hundred regular members and was hosting as many as ten contests in a month. Members also hosted contests, and the opportunities to practice forms and new ways of thought abounded. Specialty groups were added as offspring to the original group, including Twinklings for young poets, and a group of sonneteers. Vera Rich remained an active member until her death in 2009. She was a mentor, and offered her professional assistance to all members asking for special critique of their work. And, Winklings offered poets of like mind the chances they needed to begin networking all over the world.

The Winklings grew in numbers of outstanding poets writing for AllPoetry over many years. In 2009, Ron decided it was time to create and offer even more poets an opportunity to publish their works. His concept was a series of anthologies dedicated to different themes. The first set of six anthologies was called "On Viewless Wings". Ron gathered poetry hosting writing contests and offering the best poets an opportunity to be published in his anthology. He edited each volume covering six different themes, and he made large financial contributions from his own funds to make sure these anthologies were published and made available to the public at reasonable prices. It was a huge success. A planned seventh anthology in this series became the beginning of a new series, "These Human Shores," in 2012.

The birth of the International Poetry Fellowship came about in 2012 with further growth and the inevitable need for a governing body to plan, edit, market, and publish the anthologies of the new series. The first board of directors was fairly small and first chaired Mark Andrew James Terry who also helped to write the bylaws and design the cover. Our second and current chairman is Allan R. Emery (aka Joe King on AP). Allan was instrumental in gathering a larger governing group with varied business experience to become the current board of directors. Ron remained editor and anthologist, and spots opened up for directors of publishing and proofreading which filled International Poetry Fellowship poets with a strong sense of direction and business acumen in addition to poetic talents. The second volume of this series titled "These Human Shores II: The Four Corners of the Moon." Was edited by Diane Allen Hemingway. Our board of directors had grown to twelve members and the anthology improved with every new concept and publication. The third volume of this series titled: "These Human Shores III: All the World's a Stage." Was edited by Toni Christman, Diane Allen Hemingway, Lilibet Waters, Lawrence Eberhart, and Diana Sherrard-Nichols. You will find several links to places to purchase the first three books in the series throughout the IPF's website and Allpoetry Homepage, where all of the IPF's books are located in the Allpoetry Bookstore. It is our goal to produce and market world-class poetry anthologies with new and exciting themes as often as possible.

Though many of the old guard members insist on being Winklings, we are all officially members of the International Poetry Fellowship. We are a not-for-profit company of our own making, as well as loyal members of AllPoetry and try to contribute there participating in groups other than IPF, writing and reading poetry for the pure enjoyment of writing and reading, and sponsoring contests to help AllPoetry members learn and grow in this field of writing. We have a great deal of fun in our fellowship. Members have those eagerly sought, ever-growing chances to network both on AllPoetry and all over the world from meeting in an international online venue.

Each of us would like to thank you for taking time to read the story of how we came from a group of twelve poets to a group of over 275 poets who publish their work, enjoy professional leadership, and spend our time growing in a craft (or hobby as the case may be) that just might result in a career for some of us. We do hope you'll enjoy reading, "Alphabet Soup Poetry Anthology". I think you'll find some interesting new works from our regulars there. And, as always, we have new poets every year with fresh points of view.

The IPF Team

INTERNATIONAL
poetry
FELLOWSHIP

poets publishing poets

Acknowledgments

We would like to acknowledge Kevin Watt and his wonderful poetry site Allpoetry.com for creating a poetry/social vehicle which allows us to operate. It would be virtually impossible to produce our books without it. If you have not seen AllPoetry.com, do visit. Free memberships are offered.

We'd like to acknowledge Ron Wiseman, the creator/founder of the IPF, for his perseverance in creating an outstanding Poetry Publishing Group, known as the International Poetry Fellowship / (IPF).

We'd like to acknowledge all of the former and present board members of the IPF from 2012 to 2017:

During These Human Shores 1, published in 2013 - Deputy Chair: Amera Andersen-Lawson (USA), Patron: Dr. Bruce Dawe, Order of Australia, Australia, Editorial Committee: Amera Andersen-Lawson (USA), Sharon Anderson (USA), Allan Emery (USA), Diane Allen Hemingway (USA), Jocelyne Laurent (BE), Mahsa Nouraei (IRI), Ron Wiseman (AU) Membership Committee: Amera Andersen-Lawson (USA), Allan Emery (USA), Jocelyne Laurent (BE), Alison Wakefield (USA), Treasurer: Alison Emery (USA), Recording Secretary: Sharon Anderson (USA), Cover Artist: Mark Andrew James Terry (USA), Publishing Committee: Amera Andersen-Lawson (USA), Allan Emery (USA), Diane Allen Hemingway (USA), Jocelyne Laurent (BE), Alison Wakefield (USA), Cataloguist: Lisa La Grange (ZA), Series Anthologist: Ron Wiseman (AU).

During These Human Shores 2: The Four Corners of the Moon, published in late 2013: IPF Founder and Editorial Consultant: Ron Wiseman (AU), IPF Chairman: Allan R. Emery (USA), IPF Deputy Chair: Amera Andersen-Lawson (USA), Project Manager: Toni Christman (USA), Editorial Committee Chair: Diane Allen Hemingway (USA), Membership Committee Chair: Ann Copland (USA), Publishing Committee Chair: Alison Emery (USA), Treasurer: Alison Wakefield (USA), Recording Secretary: Sharon Anderson (USA), Public Communications Coordinator: Mary Boren (USA),

Lastly but not least, we'd like to acknowledge each and every single one of the talented poets whose poems are presented in Pepperoni Pizza Poetry Anthology, and all the previous IPF anthologies, These Human Shores; Volumes 1, 2 & 3, and Alphabet Soup Poetry Anthology. Without the poets, there would be no Allpoetry or IPF Anthologies.

The IPF Team

Introduction

The following poetry included in this book; Pepperoni Pizza Poetry Anthology, is a mixture of all kinds of poetry. Form Poetry, Freeverse Poetry, haiku, senryu, vignettes and all forms of Brevity Poetry. Just as you can order anything on your pizza, from Pineapple and Spam to Anchovies and Onions, (EW to me, but Yum for some!) Poetry can be written in an indefinite number of ways. All poems included in this Anthology were written by Members of the **International Poetry Fellowship**. Some Poems are Contest Winners, of various topics and styles; others are selected for publication by Board Members of the IPF, from *Allpoetry.com* Poets, as fine poetry for publication! The purpose of these Anthologies, are to create a fun social vehicle for *Allpoetry.com* Poets to publish their Poetry, In a Physical Book, as opposed to just online, and also of course, to share with any potential readers, their innermost feelings in Poetic Value. The main goals of the *IPF* are to have lots of fun publishing Poetry, and to share that Poetry with the World! We've chosen this recent theme of "Food" because there are not only a lot of fun ways to incorporate a Food theme metaphorically into Poetry, but who doesn't like food? Seriously! Food is a necessity we as humans need to consume every day to stay satisfied and alive! For poets and Poetry Lovers, Poetry is much like Food For the Soul! So Enjoy, and we hope there is a Poetic Dish, contained in these pages, which everyone can enjoy!

Allan Emery, Chairman, IPF

Gold Trophy Winners

A Wild Scudding Wind

A wild scudding wind beats
head on, hard and raw,
face and chest afire
before its strength and power
all sound but the loud howling,
carried away
in the ferocity
and tumult of the day.
The tidal pools and streams
bend before the rage
ripples riven to peaks and points
shudder and vibrate
the gale whips the calm
to fury in its wake
to set it in a palsy,
ashiver and aquake

Exhilaration of
blowing salt and water drips,
the taste of the ocean
on dry wind parched lips.
the smell of salted mud and marsh,
rocks and flailing reef
primordial smell of life
beginning in the deep
Steps become a struggle
as I smile in the glory
turning towards the maelstrom
of she the raging sea
standing tall before the ocean,
wild and full alight
and her wildly triumphant
in full orchestral flight.

Dave Kavanagh
*Gold Trophy Winner of the "Poetry of the Ocean " Contest

One Sun Rises

One sun rises
but for some there is rain,
heartbreak, sorrow, pain,
no understanding of the need
for this again,
more senseless dying,
more agony, more crying,
for someone's war, someone's
misguided hatred, someone's lying.
One sun rises
over someone's abject misery,
land of plenty living in poverty,
not everyone is rich, powerful
in the vaulted, "land of the free";
behind each scene of placid peace
someone exists who can not begin to reach,
that land of milk and honey they preach
is beyond the next horizon, so many
just wash up on the beach.
One sun rises
over mountains, plains, ocean shore,
over tenements where gangs wage war,
over inner darkness where someone wonders
if they should care anymore,
wondering if they are the only one
fighting, struggling just to see the sun,
still there is hope where hope is
a battle hard won.
And we are One,
One people, One land, One force
to be reckoned with.
We are still One,
still rising
under One Sun.

Michele Wass
*Gold Trophy Winner of the "One Today" Contest

Moon dough Pizza

I found the chef holding
the moon
In dough shape
battered to silk.
He was turning and twisting
flashing, the smooth base
into the shape of the universe!
As an onlooker, I found his
swift hand turning
like a steering wheel
his other hand was honking.
Finally, the artist placed
the base into a full moon shape.
He was smiling.

The moon was decorated
with mushroom stars
glittering stardust.
He placed a comet
a piece of clouded cheese shredded.
I found many bits of planet toppings
It looked wonderful and yummy.
when he added a sprinkle of
mars dust,
Oh,it is ready.

Smartly he pushed it into the oven
a fine spicy smell floated in the air
My mouth was a sea of saliva.
Then with a smiley
he placed my pizza in front of me
what can I say
Artist chef,
oh, you are wonderful, wonderful!

Satheesan Rangorth
Gold Trophy Winner of the "Pizza, Pizza!!" Contest

Achilles awakens

earth has an agenda
core remnants remind the oceans of deserts
without human intervention we have all of nature
from a distant star, the earth is but another ball

encircling the earth
are striations of molecules
grouped together in swirling patterns

these molecules carry genetic information
that permeates energy groups residing within
earth, air, fire and water composites

all habitation, whether it is animal, vegetable or mineral,
receive these molecules at their willful predisposition

so, if a habit-ant of earth, residing within the sphere,
has a level of awareness and engages or limits its awareness
then, the system is dependent upon all habit-ants level of awareness

In early stages of earth development
evolutionary beginnings
gave early habit-ants
greater awareness

as species increased and developed
on their evolutionary schedules of awareness
then, complications reduced the spiritual awareness,
overall within the system

and, therefore, nature fills the vacuum
and adjusts the balance on the earth
to correct imbalances

In our meatloaf earth noodle salad
tectonic plates float us to oblivion
from the comfort of our living room

we watch Mauna Loa Mauna Loa
display our insignificance

We have had all of Greek
to warn us of philosophy
overrunning our psyche

We have Rome proving
longevity eventually ends

Achilles sleeps through
end-of-Troy and wakes
to a new beginning

Michael Thomas

*Gold Trophy Winner of the "Kogi Mama!" Contest

cheesy (haiku)

hot cheesy pizza
with scorpion pepper bits
holy smoke!

Colleen Selvon-Rampersad

Gold Trophy Winner of the "Pizza, a haiku" Contest

Counting My Blessings

All that I have I am grateful for
all that I want is just greed,
upon counting my blessings I find
I have everything that I need.

Making somebody smile is amazing
giving my love is a pleasure,
being needed is always an honour
and receiving love is a treasure.

Life is all about friendship
if you're down and don't know what to do,
and you can't find someone to help
talk to someone worse off than you.

We all have our share of heartaches
blame each other for causing the pain,
but usually when we get through it
we find there is something we gain.

If God gave the gift of life
and nature provided the rest,
the least we can do is be thankful
or at least try our very best.

Norman Littleford

*Gold Trophy Winner of the "Selflessness – Why?" Contest

Silver Trophy Winners

Sounding Sea

Heart pounding, my soul exalts,
breasting great swells through moon rivered night.
Sails snap full in rolling rhythm, slacken, fill.

Green surf surging down slanting deck,
scours scuppers,
gurgling home.

Groans of straining mast increasing,
syncopated rhythm ringing
through tightening sheets and lines.

Symphonic string ensemble sounding,
Arpeggios rise through guys and stays,
Great whale whistle pierces dark night dream.

Siren song,
mistress of my being
plays for me alone.

Jack Mullen

Silver Trophy Winner of the "Poetry of the Ocean" Contest

unselfish stories

I remember sitting restless in a stuffy church on Sunday
listening to a sermon that was irrelevant to my life.
I remember the shifting bored parishioners all around me trying so
hard to avoid eye contact and anxious for the ceremony of
tediousness to end.

My thoughts went out to the sunlit park with my family spread out
on picnic tables with food and the games awaiting on the soft
summer grass dotted with blankets to lay on and fall asleep with our
stomachs full of hot dogs, pork and beans, hamburgers and all the
deserts of side dishes that were too numerous to fit into our
imaginations.

To me, that picnic was the real church and this closet of prayer with
a priest who was stupefied by an invisible god that never revealed
himself, this house-of-holiness, was the fake church.

I imagined if Jesus ever was to come back to fulfill whatever his
mandate was, he would be better off coming back to one of our
picnics and joining in with a paper plate full of good tasting food.
He would be better off laughing with Uncle Rocco shouting at his
son at the end of the table. Better off with Aunt Thelma shoving
more and more food into his dish without him even asking.

There was always a wistful sadness when the day ended and all of
us pitched in to clean up the area, putting all the trash into green
barrels that had bees and flies swarming around them.

My family was suffering from the effects of the end of World War
Two. All my uncles had served and survived the quashing of Hitler
and America saving the world from the Nazis. My family was
celebrating our small place in history as the victors over evil. Was
our society selfish? History was full of good people being killed
and cities destroyed by armies of dis-concern. Marauders of ages
past had burnt out and killed all peoples in conquered cities till all
that remained was dust.

In retrospect, was our society self indulgent and selfish over this superior attitude following the end of the war? Did all the sacrifices of soldiers dying on ill-remembered battlefields in Europe and Asia matter as a form of selfishness? We cannot surmise the full impact of history since we were too close to the event. A true learning lesson of life can only come long after the event takes place. It is if this: When we are immersed within life, we are too blind to see outside of life.

Did Jesus die on a cross as a form of selfishness? Or did Jesus go to India to study Buddhism. Did he watch as a zealot took the job on as the professed messiah to fulfill the prophecy of being the appointed one?

Did all the innocent civilians of Europe give their lives up as they fell within the range of bombs and bullets that were meant for the various soldier enemies of each other? Were those victims the un-selfish ones?

I dream of an example of a peaceful mother being pulled from her cottage home with soup on the stove and a table set for her family. I dream of her cat and dog being so mixed up over her abrupt absence. Her gardens wilting and dying from not being attended. I dream of her anguish as she is stripped, raped, thrown naked into a pit and shot and covered over with lime and dirt in the ignominious end to a life of curtailment. To me, she and all her families of a holocaust of madness, were the true people of selfishness. To those unknown unceremonious dead, I bow my head in thanks for their unselfish stories.

Michael Thomas

Silver Trophy Winner of the "Selflessness – Why? Contest

To Live As Nature Has Designed

There is a way for humankind to live organically
with no resources but whatever's naturally at hand,
relying only on the nature of the habitat
to hunt and gather, sow and reap, to clothe our nakedness,
to fashion shelters for protection from the elements,
to manufacture tools and weaponry and medicines
and even to create the implements and instruments
for graphic arts, to scribble laws and lies, to play our songs.
This way of life for humankind is known as primitive.
Although it's oftentimes romanticized in jaded minds,
it generally ensures a life that's short and lived in fear
with ignorance and prejudice regarding everything
beyond ancestral knowledge and one's tribal heritage.

When individuals unburdened by their fears and pride
are given opportunities to choose conveniences
derived from human ingenuity and enterprise
in social paradigms of cultural complexity,
they almost always choose a way of life more civilized.
When they have seen how agriculture and a husbandry
achieved through sharing science and economies of scale
improves the true sustainability of food supplies,
subsistence living tends to lose appeal it might have had.
They choose careers and jobs above communal roles assigned
and exercise their curiosity in broader fields.
They soon discover very little in the wider world
is in the trees or on the ground to simply use or eat,
and that the natural world is challenged to accommodate
technologies to feed and clothe and house and entertain
the billions of humanity in ever longer lives.
But if they get a broader sense of human history,
they find the earth survives the foibles of the human race.

For human beings all around the world learn every day
in fits and starts, by errors made and small successes won
how better to cooperate in earth's complexity
of global economics, cultural activity

and nature's fragileness but ultimate resiliency.
Our species with its intellect and ingenuity
arose from nature and is part of nature's own design.
We vex our Mother, Nature, in the way that children do.
But if and as the human race continues to mature,
we shall become what nature always meant for us to be.
More people then may have a broader view of history
regarding humankind in nature's marvelous design.
Eschewing lives wherein we starve and shiver in the dark,
we shall pursue our natural destiny, compelled to live
on earth as true to our design as all creation is.

Ben Mosley

Silver Trophy Winner of the "Kogi Mama" Contest

mozzarella (haiku)

mozzarella
strings from lips
delicioso

Vivacious

Silver Trophy Winner of the "Pizza, a haiku" Contest

Old Soul

Fourteen-thousand, two-hundred,
fifty-eight moons have looked down
from the sky upon my life's breath.
So contrite when I add experience,
broken hearts, an absent mother
and death.

I've wandered around
the life I've been given
and asked a million questions.
I've breathed sighs
beneath the stars
to search out
just where I'm driven.

I'm derived from dust...
molecular matter.
The skin and bones I'm in
have become a lasting footprint
of carbon-data
on the mend.

More often than not I classify
the bad as the good
and I know some things
I've done are wrong
but I wouldn't change it if I could.

Love is just a four letter word
I've come to depend upon
where compromise and understanding
makes waves in the rattled con.

A figment here, a cell there
molecular homicide.
When will it all stop?
Well not until I've died.

A tremble is the damn-dest thing
it can make or break a soul.
Let me tell you, if any I should know.
How fast I've gotten old!

You think I'm young
when you count those moons
but I tell you that I'm ancient.
I have seen more in my life
than most have learned
and will forget.

Bobbie Jean Wright

Silver Trophy Winner of the "Great Poet Impersonations" Contest

A Single Slice (Rondeau)

A single slice of crusted pizza dough
distends a starving gut to not let go.
With vital veggies baked to take away,
one morsel beats a meal of mash today;
it's daily doses make a garden flow.

You roll wheat flour, gently toss and throw.
The baking batter must not overflow
before the fixing flavors yield warm way,
a single slice.

One earth abounds with nature's bounty glow,
the sun shines light on ground to feed below.
Those stricken faces see the sky display
a hope that on this blessed given day
the pie is sliced with nutrients that grow
a single slice.

Laurie F. Grommett
Silver Trophy Winner of the "Great Poet Impersonations" Contest

Imitation

On the northern outskirts of Milan
on a dim Sunday in June,
the rain dampened the cobblestones
but not my mood.
I was hungry for adventure;
Antonio was just hungry.

"What's good around here?"
I asked Legnano's native son.

"Everything, it's Italy," he chuckled
with a superior grin that I could not refute
and one of his countless hand gestures
like tossing me an imaginary ball.

So far, the cuisine of my hosts
had been stellar.
Whether in a trattoria
for a quick sandwich
of squaquerone and prosciutto,
or an adventurous meal of elk
in a four-star restaurant,
the chefs of Northern Italy
had not failed to impress.

Three weeks in Lombardy
and I had avoided all the clichés
but I suddenly had a craving.
"Pizza?" I ventured.
"The best in the world!" he promised.

Mind you,
I'm rather a connoisseur of 'za.
I held in high esteem
the gooey, thick creations
delivered to my doorstep
by earnest high-school boys.

But naturally, as this was the land
where the humble pie was born,
I was amenable to the prospect,
though skeptical:
Could anything beat a Pizza Hut
Pan Supreme with Extra Cheese
and Bacon-Stuffed, Garlic Rolled
Crust, golden brown, dipped in Ranch
and washed down with a Bud?

Off we skittled in a tiny Fiat
to Al Borgo Antico,
a restaurant his friend owned.
Antonio suggested that we each order one
and choose according to our palates.
For my part, salami, onions,
mushrooms and tomatoes fit the bill.
Antonio ordered "frutti di mare,"
a seafood extravaganza.
"That's not pizza. Fish doesn't go on pizza.
Except anchovies. And they're gross.
But whatever," my inner monologue came.
And I worried about any pizzeria
That offered mussels as a topping.

The proprietor, Giovanni,
brought each one over himself
and they were things of beauty:
enormous discs of crispy crust, cracker thin,
so big they'd have fed Caesar's legions,
and topped with the requisite ragù,
Italy's finest cheeses,
and all the garnishes we'd ordered.

Like Adam at the Tree of Knowledge,
one bite and I knew the truth:
fast-food factory delivery creations

back in America
would never again suffice,
for I had tasted Italy,
and I was ruined.

Milan is a memory now
and Antonio is an ocean away.
But sometimes on a rainy day,
I bake my own pizza:
simple thin-crust, tangy marinara,
garlic, mozzarella, oregano.
Try as I might, I'll never be Giovanni,
but my creations bring back
the flavor of mirth,
and as the sauce drips
from the corner of my upturned mouth
my tongue bats it back in
for fear of losing even a morsel
of the memory.

Thomas Horton

Silver Trophy Winner of the "Pizza, Pizza!!" Contest

Bronze Trophy Winners

Turmoil

We all become dust. Wars scar the living,
no matter which side. The winners reward:
they get to write history.
Love like the sun touches everyone;
some, still, layer on many conversations
to keep it from touching them. Vulnerability
only leads to hurt. We, who love
freely, realize rejection is not about us.
Ice chills the drink. The currents in the ocean,
life's shifts and challenges depend on contrast.
We think of winter and the laughter in snow when
summer heat and humidity are melting us.
Those heavily clothed in mountain heights know
when the sun is scorching overhead, move carefully,
for ice hangs heavy as it melts and what is smooth
now is often slicker than when frozen. We are never
safe, yet we fool ourselves as often as we can.
What lives on the inside is what shows up
in the world we live in. Perhaps when we learn
to no longer be at war with ourselves, when we accept
the kaleidoscope of feelings and thoughts our minds create
we will no longer want everyone to agree with us,
demand consistency in a grainy and turbulent world.
Peace is not a still pond, except for brief moments.
We end as certain as every effort has its cost.
How we "be" as we get there is all we can control.
No one else is responsible for our happiness;
joy expresses itself in the sharing of love. We
are never going to serve ourselves or our life as hermits.
No matter how long the truisms rain down upon us,
we shall sleep in conflict and hatred until unwilling
to define ourselves by what we are against. You can
never tell me what something is
by telling me what it isn't.

Thomas Burson
*Bronze Trophy Winner of the "One Today" Contest

after life's latest storm

Washed ashore
spent creature of the land
lost at sea
at sea
lost
beached
instead of drowned
laying on a flat thin edge of life
covered with sand.

And why
as though recovery were an option
did the sea spit me out?
Surely not for my sake.
Was the sea too full for this morsel
left to drift so close
along the edge
raspy voiced pile
so barely breathing
along this mile
of lonely shore?
A single further wave
could snuff the candle out
leaving bleached bones
for the windy years to store.

In the balance
hanging
in this rippling deliberation
contemplating catlike
my end
and I care not
emotions having bled out
staining but faintly
too anemic for much ado
as pale as the wrinkled skin
blue lipped hue.

Sucker punching life has waylaid
body and soul
as another wave gives a roll
and laps
gently
again
again
playing
deciding
if it wants me
after all
back in.

Don Skidmore

Bronze Trophy Winner of the "Poetry of the Ocean" Contest

Life's sweetest lessons

I shall not seek for understanding,
it's best thou stand for what thou see.
The way I view the wheel that's turning,
be the only thing to take with me.

I shall not dwell upon thy judgments,
of angry men with scores of grief,
nor taste of ripeness should they faulter,
yet pray thy lesson brings relief.

I shall not gloat on challenges conquered,
or perch oneself on lofty throne.
Shall always heed another failure,
for such a turn demands me, grow.

I shall not run onto the morrow,
to catch a dream with soul in tow.
Moreover,
shalt up ones sails,
and set my heart upon thy way winds blow.

I shall not give way to grief nor sorrow
for a seed of love did birth their growth.
And if to die upon thy morrow,
smile I plead,
and honour thy oath.

I shall not trust onto the mirror,
for that on which my name be shown.
For in the glass of eternal dwellings,
thy mirror holds ten thousand pains unknown.

I shall not react upon your action,
that mask was never kind on me,
I'd sooner walk away the fallen
than question ones integrity.

I shall not demand a love that's chained,
thy currency be free to flow,
I'll always honour honesty
for thy weeping willow once said, No.

I shall not curse the changing weathers,
the earth she cries I feel her pain.
Raffish, I'll don my smile cap n'feather.
not matter hail, sun,
wind or rain

This gift of life has been a blessing,
that through which do humbly stray.
Every step I've walked a lesson
for life tastes much the sweeter this way.

Matthew Bower

Bronze Trophy Winner of the "Selflessness – Why?" Contest

Thin crust (haiku)

thin crust
in a world away from Napoli
spam and pineapple

Paul Geiger

*Bronze Trophy Winner of the "Pizza, a haiku" Contest

When In Rome...

I grew up in little Italy.
Yes, it's sits on the US map,
singing home of The Four Seasons.
Saucy spaghetti met meatball
and gave birth to cheesy pizza flap.

Since Belleville, New Jersey
was part of the garden state,
red and green tomato vines grew
on Momma Mia's front porch.
Three pies served a group of eight.

Toppings were traditional:
pepperoni, mushrooms, onions,
kalamatas, anchovies   on the side.
Three cheeses were expected.
We ate on paper plates on the piazza,
came in for TV reruns.

I know you reread my last two lines
and said what? I grew up in little Italy
in a kosher home where "traif"
was not permitted inside,
but dietary rules never stopped my family.

When in Rome we did as the Romans did.

Laurie F. Grommett

Bronze Trophy Winner of the "Pizza, Pizza!!" Contest

For Evermore.

When all else fails
interest abates,
when the mountain
Is climbed,
when crippled knees
take my love of dance,
I write...
When love is stolen,
and darkness shadows me,
when dogs girt my sanity,
I write...
Writing takes me inly,
it challenges, provokes,
releases, fulfils, connects...
It is kind to me when I'm old,
brazen indelible and bold.
An impossibility of torn pages
laid bare, screwed and cast
'midst long piled floors,
compiled thoughts
for evermore...

William Rout

Bronze Trophy Winner of the "Great Poet Impersonations" Contest

HM Trophy Winners

The Mermaid's Retreat

On silver oceans touching sky
Where water spirits soar on high
Dawn casts her magic mantle wide,
And drives the ocean world alive.

White horses reach the beach in rows
They frisk and leap to ride the foam,
Aloft in joyous glee they prance
Joining the joyous, oceanic dance.

But best is when Mermaids appear
In raiment's spun from angel tears
Which glisten as resplendent scales,
Adorning every shimmering tail.

Singing songs in magical verse
To lull the nights inclement curse,
Oh such a wondrous sight is this
In early morning's briny mist.

Bev Pollard

*HM Trophy Winner of the "Poetry of the Ocean" Contest

haiku

dust storm rises
in the distant horizon
pizza dough

Madhu Singh

*HM Trophy Winner of the "Pizza, a haiku" Contest

Small Expectations

Too often we search
The various shades of breath,
Meditate upon the philosophy of stars
that contour our destiny's cartography,
too often epiphany comes
through silver tips of hair, when by then
we tend to broken quills,
ravaging to ink the chronicles of life;

that essence of truth and theory of life
opens itself in the littlest of things,
charity lies not in the sun,
but in the tiny sparks of fireflies' glint,
the moments we ignored to love of self,
now surging the conscience in shots of regret,

each gesture of appreciation you strove to make,
the smile that throbbed from a sober heart,
the note of thanks you scribbled on chit,
the warmth of hug to the coldest soul,
the pat on the back to the discouraged spirit,
the surprise rose on a rainy day,
the silent sacrifice of unspoken words,
the midnight oil that burned for a friend,
the prayer that melted the enemy's heart,

these the deeds of selflessness explained,
the drops of love that sanctify our cross,
compassion lies not in the complexities
but innocent renderings of a childlike heart,
too often we realize at the ripened age,
the folly of a child that is laughed upon,
rained upon man the pearls of wisdom.

Rupa Thomas

HM trophy Winner of the "Selflessness – Why?" Contest

Kogi Mam's Kin

And we the Kogi Mama's kin,
Did hear the word and feel the sin,
Intransigence and bonehead acts,
Accentuate the Kogi facts;
Descended they from mountains high,
From whence the voice within the sky
Demanded we curtail our toil,
Destruction of the native soil;
We rape the earth and reap the trees,
Ignore the local natives' pleas,
The greed is all for us to see,
And we are king, forever free
To here destroy our garden hence,
Devoid of all good common sense.

Alistair Muir

*HM Trophy Winner of the "Kogi Mama" Contest

Without cheese (haiku)

without cheese
there are no strings attached
pizza girl

Kasi Senghor

*HM Trophy Winner of the "Pizza, a haiku" Contest

Read Me

I'm just a writer
when no one reads anymore

who'd read me

I write measured by moments of other's bedlam
and mine
words pulling at my temples before the train comes to a stop
in my thoughts
as life moves on like
it's in a hurry

read me
read me now
read me then
read me in between

but read me goddammit

feel the words bite
watch them drizzle
down the page
hear a quiet scream
as it bursts out of your mouth
quite unintended

just read me

Diane Gwynne Allen

*HM Trophy Winner of the "Great Poet Impersonations" Contest

The Ebb and Flow

I sit near the water's edge,
with sun peeking through
the clouds overhead and
waves washing sand
upon the shore.

Just for now,
I am caught up
in the ebb and flow;
the timeless pattern
of the seas.

My taught muscles relax;
the tension washed
away with the
receding currents,
oblivious to time.

I close my eyes;
listen to the
ocean sounds,
sift grains of sand
between my fingers.

Soon I must leave,
concede to restraints of time
and life filled conflict;
the ocean and sand
respite for only a day.

Sue K. Green

*HM trophy Winner of the "Poetry of the Ocean" Contest

Isn't such love a gift of the Lord?

Isn't magic of love a mom who selflessly cares?
Supplicates for her child tearfully in her prayers.

Begs God to bless her cherub with a lasting cure,
Of illnesses and disabilities a sick child endures.

Not knowing if her little one would ever get well,
Listens to all kinds of healers whatever they tell.

Trying every remedy hoping it will restore health,
Even if in return she has to give up all her wealth.

Devotes her entire life expecting nothing in return,
Even when she is too old, it would still be her turn.

For such a handicapped child, to always look after,
A dependent baby with only a body growing bigger.

The mind staying tiny as when tying umbilical cord,
Isn't such mother's love the greatest gift by the Lord?

Dr. Asghar Nazeer

HM Trophy Winner of the "Selflessness - Why?" Contest

The Bluebird

Only at night
Do I hear the bluebird sing
Only then,
Do I allow his song.

Despair has filled my days.
Since I were a child
Challenged me,
At every turn.

Poetry, I tried
Wrote it down
Even then
No one listened.

Whiskey became my staff
Drowning reality
Each day, unto
The next.

I do not allow
The bluebird here.
He belongs in the night,
Both of us free.

Sue K. Green

HM Trophy Winner of the "Great Poet Impersonations" Contest

always more

I

the eyes of younger brother stare into the world
like beads proudly pontificating over
its own creation, wanting more

the eyes of younger brother like eyes of a beetle
have little humanity left and are driven by entitlement
a self-perpetuating hunger for more

empty eyes of younger brother will encroach slowly
like a demented diseased jaguar stocking its prey
obliviously mocking warnings of what's in store

bottomless eyes of younger brother glare with envy
losing empathy with each slight inconvenience
devising ways around his conscience to rape more
always more

II

the seven billion pairs of eyes
you best not catch them staring
don't fall into their empty lies
for you they're never caring

for you they will build a reserve
and teach your children to want
so when broken they will all serve
the heartless machine they flaunt

younger brother will buy the land
and your culture will be sold
few if any will take a stand
while you are left in the cold

then the myriad of others

will so easily ignore
the desperate elder brothers
to receive what they want… more
always more

Dayenoble

*HM Trophy Winner of the "Kogi Mama" Contest

Blackbird

Morning friend in garments plain
slips into the garden unseen
flits from bed to bed in turn
to breakfast on some grub or worm
and once he claims this repast
repays the tenants rent in part
with music from his golden horn
he whistles magic to the morn
and perched on twig with full chest
his song will far out do the rest
for what he lacks in silver and gold
He gives instead of tune so bold
the creator made him dull and dark
but gave him voice of some remark
with his song he will praise the lord
our morning friend the Blackbird

Dave Kavanagh

*HM trophy winner of the "Selflessness – Why?" Contest

Bright Eyes

I doubt you've noticed, but
I find myself searching for something;
Something I never thought possible.
I climbed a mountain and found transcendence.
I witnessed a beauty I never dreamt to exist.

There on the mountain I saw a sea of green,
A viridescent ocean reaching out to the horizon.
And there, where the sea and heavens met,
Were islands of black, filled with lights.
Stars began to appear.

They came to watch the islands, the sea,
And me upon the mountain.
I took a breath of air shared with stars,
And as its purity and perfection filled my lungs,
I was immersed in sublimity.

As I faced the elegance and grace of His creation,
My heart began to bloom.
In that moment,
that fragment of time,
I was filled.

I was filled
with warmth, with utter plenitude.
I was blessed with just a taste
of true grace,
nourishing the depths of my spirit.

Now, if you let your mind imagine
And capture this sense of elation,
You will only begin to understand
What it is that I've seen.
So, I find myself searching,
Longing to find that mountain once more.

That sip of beauty that fills the human soul.
I visit that mountain every night, and from my pillow
I witness the sea, island lights, and stars again,
Only for them to fade into the morning rays.

Stephen W. Peake

*HM Trophy Winner of the "Poetry of the Ocean" Contest

cheesy moon (haiku)

cheesy moon
makes Hawaiian smile
tropical slice

Penelope Allen

*HM trophy winner of the "Pizza, a haiku" Contest

Cheese drizzles

cheese drizzles
over pizza sauce
addiction

CrimsonDew / Firdous Arjuman

*HM Trophy Winner of the "Pizza, a haiku" Contest

Why Is A Heart Pulled Aside

No sadder thing than longing -
tonight my mind caresses dark's distraught
breath's contour that languors deep
where opal-teardrops flow
where the year of the heart thinks of snow
without the warming sun
everything grows cold
in this place of sorrowing.

If only I could that love would come again
that fragrant mistress with faintings smooth,
she without cure
ere lost to failing
ere left so sad
bereft of color
withered and wailing.

Why is a heart pulled aside
falling wide ?

I grope memories
where clouds would part
the moon's thickness -
the veil diminished

I shivered amid the wound.

Why weave such lutes
the windsong deeds have been undone,
the bale-blight secret-groan of doom
the blue-malediction's deft of skill
where scorn rests upon my affliction

the hand that hurts all tenderness,
shunning grace of compassion's pulse

it's all she could give -
her love no longer full.

And in the shadows
whatever was done
the smear seeped from light that fails
the night without end
the fading mood sheds.

I wanted to believe,
but more the same
says the lonely breeze. .. .

there's nothing else ahead.

Far'way strands of time and lonely-lore
with tired eyes, dim and weeping
mid the realms as bliss did fade -
the withered amaranth died today
the lyre once wreathed
blooms upon cheeks have now departed,
scored and sorrowed
every road wandered.. .
bound for woodland's brown.

O dearest misery
plight that bears the measure
each whisper through blades of grass
we beg return
but the heart has vanished.

O Dear,
you cry 'long the bluer moon
you look as bruised this tender hour. .. .
you were to be remembered,
once pristine, you'd been delivered
as we had known. .. .

such days have grown so old.

R. D. Stone

HM Trophy Winner of the "Kogi Mama" Contest

A place to dwell

Her dreams
flicker soft
casting dimly lit
shadows
on her wishes
to fly

Her candle of hope
illuminating
the pallid corners
shrinking
ever so swiftly
granting panic
a place to dwell

limping forward
to the sea

Maria Oday

HM Trophy Winner of the "Poetry of the Ocean" Contest

Love Un-delayed

Over at neighbor's I look I see
a wife performing husbandry
The man her senior does not fret
with her as she toils in dry or wet

Morn to eve she's tireless at work
never a day's duty does she shirk
She gives her all in summer in fall
and only prosperity comes to call

When, as expected, the man falls sick
there she is, his walking stick
I read once where there will often be
a woman to keep man's company
but ladies can't expect such sympathy

I found in their story, glory of giving
and wished their example upon the living
Her selflessness is not commonplace
full of compassion, face mirroring grace

Today is no different, a Sunday no less
I hear her brush-cutting, raking with zest
from there to the kitchen manna displayed
acts which inspire love un-delayed
I watched, I saw I prayed

kasi senghor

HM Trophy Winner of the "Selflessness – Why?" Contest

And Then I Die

Such an ease for life, almost unfair,
assuaged an ego that would age
with no benefactor or grace.
The melodrama of existence
that was incessantly spat upon me,
initially at work where I could feign concern
while my warped and selfish id belched with laughter,
soon stalked my departure and many nights awakened
me with its callus laughter at the irony of my bravado.

In time the interminable act found no intermission
and simply tagged along, making no effort at subversion,
goading my shuffling gait and apathetic shoulders
barely supporting a heavy head
that was more than once a hair's breadth
from fragmentation
and an after-the-fact note
that would be only a pathetic attempt
of a madman to justify insanity.

So many nights their laughter and glee
were the scabbard in my already weeping wound.
How does angst bear such joie de vivre?
No cross to bear, but I was suspended nonetheless
by self-imposed ligatures of expectation.
The impulses often pushed decisions hellhound,
where I'd resided so many times before
I'm certain a permanent residence was awaiting.

It's not about me.
So many times I heard it that it became dogma,
with perhaps more than splinter of truth
jammed beneath my middle finger's nail
on display to any who would care.

Only an ego of such epic proportion
could suppress the reflexive drive to destruction

that fueled my every waking moment.
God damn the day,
I'm a darkness addict.
Light illuminates, denies the covert and uproots
the subterfuge until it is exposed and shriveled in the heat
of reality's unyielding beams.

I created the world that I could manipulate
but I cannot direct the variables.
Control is the ultimate power,
and only with pen can I fight opinion and criticism.
My words dribble silently.

I must die,
that is a given.
I have fought death's calling
so long that life now assumes a semblance
of normalcy.
I have reproduced,
I have given life,
and I have deceived all them all.
I don't deserve to live,
and I don't desire to die,
at least not yet, not now by my hand.
Though the quick and easy
would be the most fulfilling,
I shall endure whatever fate has in mind
and rid myself of control at least
before I go.
Death on death's terms
sounds fine to me,
finally.

James Nichols

HM Trophy Winner of the "Great Poet Impersonations" Contest

The Last Note

I.

I have gone out
and I don't see well anymore.

I have gone out.
There is no desire for the ego
to meet the great inflator.

Children's toys of size don't
fascinate me, even when they try
to scratch the sky, equate size with age.

I have gone out

II.

and the railroad is rusting.
A thin line
for sunsets to follow. My brother's
agonizing over the death of steam; my son
the death of diesel. And they trace their dreams
on the rust trails, as they polish their living room
miniatures.

III.

The cars have buried New Jersey.
It sank, becoming
the Atlantic's first coral reef. My generation
of venerators call it a psychic phenomenon,
a phantasy equal to New York.
(Children's toys have a way of escaping the living room.
The toys, wait in corners, breathing dreams to the child's
tactile senses. And when he toy meets she toy,
they complete the living tactile sense) Green
image of a forest,
the reflected image of car paint.

IV.

Who am I to write
the great American Epic?
There is no great American Epic.
We don't have time for it -- as we wrap
the continent with strings, each one
pulling tighter -- we try for a puppet master's
control of understanding. (Agonized
by the obliteration of the sun
every day. I watch it, fascinated.
As it burns itself to death.)

I have gone out.

There is no Great American Epic for me. Perhaps,
a greater metropolitan epic or
a greater suburban epic but,
housewives have cried over most of them, used them
as seasoning for nuptial understanding. (Who has time
to physically masturbate, these days. Ginsberg's dirty
old man died with the "informed youth of today")
There is no greater American Epic, no film
to profit off it's attitude.

V.

I have gone out,
so has my next door neighbor,
and the black cats in the ghettos
who I don't understand.

We've all gone out.
Agony being essential for progress.
There is nothing more.
Just go out
Just go out
And face it.

VI.
(I just got stoned by a child's toy. Is that legal?)

March 4, 1969
dedicated to Jocelyn Browne

Thomas N. Burson

HM Trophy Winner of the "Kogi Mama" Contest

mozzarella (haiku)

mozzarella melts
on a bright Tuscan caper
four degrees off plumb

cuul / Cliff Lindemann

Ode to Cold Pizza

Just the thought of you as I lay my head down
finds a smile on my face
tonight you satisfied all my late night cravings
my mouth waters at the idea of your sausage!
As I drift off
my mind contented
knowing what's left of our evening together
awaits me in the morn
your always better for breakfast

Maria Oday

HM Trophy Winner of the "Pizza, Pizza!!" Contest

Tikkun

To whom am I a tragedy
that demands stillness?
and in that stillness
must drink spirits of regret.

These four cubits
long vulnerable
seem stunted, and stifle
my hands to affect change.

Free me from shackles
I pray
from binding ropes and
tethered dreams

From treacheries committed--
immoral incarnations
of slight--
from fear and stillness.

From the overt-ness of this human
condition
unbind. That I may hold these hands
outward;
the sick to heal,
the lame to know walking,
the hungry to fill.

There are locked cupboards
overfull
with food and medicine--
but I have no key.

David N. Betzer

*HM Trophy Winner of the "Selflessness – Why?" Contest

Ashawari

the mirage is
you are
listening to this tune,
in reality the tune is
much more,
it's a song,
an evening Raga
Yaman Kalyan
played on Sarod,
a mid-night raga
Malkaus
played on Sitar,
ashawari
played in morning
in a flute or violin
dwindling between
hopes and despair
resembling your pain;

this is Tagore
singing aloud
in your heart,
Nazrul speaking
for unification
of two Bengals,
calling loud
for revolution;
the tabla
in rapid fingers
of Alla Rakha
creating the sound
of marching soldiers
on horse back
with open bayonets:

it is Bukowski
visiting a brothel

to know their pain
first hand
and stunned to find
a lover of his poems
who can share a night
gratis
in exchange for
a poem, a true picture of life;

the tiger roars
in the Sunder-bans
crocodile tears are shed
in the banks of
the Ganges, the Brahmaputra,
the Satlej and the Kaveri
the Brahmins alone
with meticulous perception
pronounce the slokas
mixing all waters together
but the minds, the hearts
of millions rotate
in different directions
bringing bloodshed
in the name of
language, religion;

yet day turns to evening
evening to night
with the promise of
another golden morning
when we know not
whether we will see it
or at least our
next generation.

Rajkumar Mukherjee

HM Trophy Winner of the "Great Poet Impersonations" Contest

Indian Summer

Neither whisper nor revelation rose
When summer slipped the autumn equinox;
Warm winds sheared the shepherds and their flocks,
Turned the damned that dangled from the gallows;
Birds arrowed over open plain,
Yet did not seed the clouds with rain;
No downpour muted creaking weathercocks.

The young still loved with reckless vows of spring;
Buds fresh against the soil, too frail for frost,
Leafed upward, claiming moments winter lost;
Scarecrows like saviors kept crops from withering;
The sea alone beneath the sun,
Alive with arctic expectation,
Declined to breach the cusp the season crossed.

Deeper waters have forgotten heat;
Sunken canyons mark the colder currents,
Glacial scars of ancient permanence
Grown numb against the constant thermal heartbeat,
Wounds which ground to silt the rocks
Of megaliths from early epochs
Forever lost within the liquid silence.

The ocean held us once, but we were wild;
We shed our skin and crawled from its cocoon
To dance with spears beneath the harvest moon
And bleed the lesser beasts the gods exiled;
We broke the forest wall with fire,
Savored the marrow of an empire;
With idle oaths we turned our backs on Neptune.

The sun replaced the sea and flamed our heart;
We left the moon to tinker with the tide,
Grew drunk on wine and song, and filled with pride
We built up what the ocean tore apart,

But doubt consumed the minds of men
When wind and ice returned again,
And strange and pitiless gods were deified.

Little of love weds cold, yet there is beauty,
Not in death but dying: the ancient baptism,
The clarity of distance, the twilight of Sodom.
It is a siren's call which draws from duty
Men who would be cast as heroes
To name the stars which stain the cosmos
And carve their course beside the rib of Adam.

Season fell to season in its turn;
Ice formed and faded to mark each passing year;
Flowers bloomed and withered then reappeared;
Life lumbered on, but we who dreamt were stubborn,
Heirs unwilling to embrace
The routine of this lazy pace:
We toppled idols worshiped out of fear.

Even the cold-blooded which sun on stone
Understand the warmth within the field
As love, a love the winter months concealed,
One nursed in light the moon has never known;
We are, in mind, a loftier breed,
No nobler in truth: we, too, concede
The richer soul as one that heat has healed.

The long days filled with kindling, filled with flint;
We gathered driftwood washed up on the shore,
And lit again the ancient watchtower,
Drove forth the multitudes red and violent
To turn the earth, to dig fresh tombs,
To pierce the dark and muted wombs,
Seeking warmer rivers to baptize our savior.

William Kenneth Keller

HM Trophy Winner of the "Poetry of the Ocean" Contest

Neath Silvered Moon

I shucked my shoes, in bare feet walked
along the moonlit beach,
and listened as the breezes spoke
in softly murmured speech,
the crashing waves played tympani
with drum rolls made of brine,
and rippled notes of harmony
danced cancan's chorus line.
Long braids of tresses splayed upon
cragged rocks that lined the shore,
deriding efforts of the tide
to pilfer kelps décor,
and pungent pools of low tide fame
were cleansed by saline spray,
as limpets clung tenaciously
in midnight's calm soiree.

Shy hermit crabs played hooky as
they sidle through the sand,
small starfish made short dashes, to
and from shore's hinterland,
old driftwood basks in silvered beams
of lunar mystic glow,
just waiting for the tide to catch
their bulk in undertow.
The tang of salt tastes on my lips,
and rests inside my clothes,
wet grains of sand are squished between
the fissures of my toes,
when I look back my footprints are
erased from midnight's scene,
and with them gone, it's just as if
this stroll has never been.

Alf Collier

*HM Trophy Winner of the "Great Poet Impersonations" Contest

One

Conflicts, conflicts, conflicts
Within me, outside me, it inflicts
The ones deep inside of me
troubles the most you see

I sit here with closed eyes
oblivious of all that's nice
Holding together all that shatters
nothing around really matters

My mind, my body, my soul - all still
sitting on a rock, letting silence drill
I sense a newfound freedom
in the rarest peaceful kingdom

I listen to my breath, resting tongues
inhale pristine air into my lungs
I feel that positive energy
spread through my body gathering synergy

I exhale with all might and force
expelling the origin of negative source
I flush all the impurities that are shoddy
I can feel it drain and leave my body

I smell that tree within me when I breathe
I no more sense the hard rock underneath
I feel my purified reflection in reverse
I am ONE, with the universe

Sanjay Sudheendran AKA AquaHeart

*HM Trophy Winner of the"Selflessness-Why?" Contest

One Veggie Pizza Delight

We have one today
perhaps another tomorrow
but what we do with today
creates happiness or sorrow

I lift mine eyes
towards the hills
to gaze upon
Purple Majesty's appeal

High atop
one fruited plain
one prayer ascend
brought forth one rain

One father
one mother
one moon
one sun

One today
one people
one prayer
tomorrow does come

One sky beneath
one heaven today
one wind to blow
one ground to play

One history
one theme
one people
one dream

We are all one together
beneath one sky

one veggie pizza delight
on rye

One country
one home
one people do show
one name to find
together we grow

Hearthrob DaPoet

*HM Trophy Winner of the "One Today" Contest

Pizza

In
Pizza
Rules do
Not exist. If
You wish, a cookie
Can become a pizza. Yes,
This is true. Any flavor you choose.

A
Great
Pizza pie
Is deep dish,
Layer it high. Top
The pizza with ham and
Pineapples. Add crushed
Bacon and three kinds of cheese.
Six inches thick, layered gratification.

Arianna Aleshire

*HM Trophy Winner of the "Pizza, Pizza!!" Contest

"Mama Rosas, A Taste Of Italy"

In New Orleans when it came time
to hold a fundraiser for the Center
we knew who to ask to serve as hosts.
Since those of us recovered were the
backbone of the business,
how could they say, "No?"

Second floor above the pizzeria
was a cavernous space just right
for the boys to perform on the sturdy
stage.

All the drag one could stand,
spaghetti and pizza included,
five dollars at the door,
see the man.

Pent up energy from sobriety,
fired the acts,
frenzied to levels that nosebleeds
gave one pause, this was serious.

If we were lucky, the stars
reemerged from exile,
rekindling lost fame,
their classics from the past.

Like "A Night To Remember,"
with mercy from the gods,
our potential Titanic did not sink
while the band played on.

A few wigs sailed, a broken heel
or two, but nothing compared to
weekends before the well ran dry
for the fortunate few.

Another six months in the black,
pepperoni power, worshiped
like manna,
shared by the masses.

Those nights gave us hope
and the joy to believe
we could all be family
once again.

James C. Allen

*HM Trophy Winner of the "Pizza, Pizza!!" Contest

Pizza

Monday, Tuesday, Wednesday too,
PIZZA dinners just for you.
Thursday, Friday, Sunday all
Get ready for the pizza call.

Thin crust, tomato sauce,
cheese just right;
six days' dinners
prove quite a delight.

Sue K. Green

*HM Trophy Winner of the "Pizza, Pizza!!" Contest

the crust i knead

the crust i knead
the crust- i NEED
the garlic scented bliss
and when there is that cheese inside-
a donkey i would kiss
for just a taste, a little bite
of that hot pizza pie,
i love it classic, topped with cheese,
or wild, piled high-
with sausage, jalapenos,
and pineapple to the sky!

The pizza is the perfect food,
the pyramid served round,
or even square, well,
i don't care- as long it's mouth bound!
The slippery grease of pizza chains
or basil, green and fresh,
red sauce that took ma days to make
- the rest are flavourless!

So thank you, those italians
who ran out of bread dough,
who took the time, to roll it out,
without you i'd be in woe,
bless your hearts (and pizzas too)
and do the pizza thing you do!

Emilija Morkunaite

*HM Trophy Winner of the "Pizza, Pizza!!" Contest

Semi-Finalists

till you awake

Hibernating soon, your world's sun
slumber seeping, peace has begun.
Brush me with essence of your breasts
that I may dream upon our rests.

How I endure love's lonely day
lavender blue tide turns grey.
Lie with me on Golden Rock's edge
whisper words of lover's pledge.

For seventeen of moons I'll fast
no morsel till the days have passed.
Sweet kisses bathe your eyelash close
Linger on mouth, desirous rose.

Listen to clash of bubbly foam
awaiting joys of ocean's roam.
Where in world would I rather be
than lovers' embrace, you and me?

Colleen Selvon-Rampersad

*Semi-Finalist of the "Poetry of the Ocean" Contest

The Mermaid

By the shore on midnight,
while singing to the moon...
She heard a mermaid humming,
a song without a tune...

She saw the mermaid beckon,
pointing in the air...
While slipping in the ocean,
without a thought, or care...

As she slipped beneath the water,
feeling the slippery sand...
Laughing with the mermaid,
while swimming, hand in hand...

The moonlight scattered diamonds,
as the waves crashed on the shore...
while barely feeling bottom,
on this slippery, ocean floor...

She heard the mermaid humming,
a song without a tune...
But the mermaid wasn't swimming,
as she lay now on the dune...

As she swam beneath the water,
to the ocean's sandy shore...
She heard the mermaid laughing,
like she didn't laugh before...

The dawn was breaking softy,
as she glanced back towards the sea...
for the mermaid that was laughing,
was just the other...me...~

Melody Hamby Goss
Semi-Finalist of the "Poetry of the Ocean" Contest

Dance Of Dawn

The gentle waves are breaking 'pon
The sandy stretch of shore
Below the hues of brilliant dawn
Where seagulls swiftly soar
Upon the wind as zephyr sighs
To welcome start of day
And whispers soothing lullabies
To stow the night away.

Carnation floods horizons breadth
Reflecting off the sea
As luminescence floods the depths
With sweet serenity
To paint a lustrous tapestry
In nature's morphing hue
That mimics throes of ecstasy
As day makes rendezvous.

The palms are casting silhouettes
Across the sands expanse
As spume performs and pirouettes
Entranced in morning's dance
While eyes awake to view the scene
Enveloping the skies
Where azure dots the vibrant skein
That seeks to hypnotize.

Dave Hartford

Semi-Finalist of the "Poetry of the Ocean" Contest

Ocean Lessons

A sea shell whispers ocean's roar
when held closely to open ear.
Because the sound is stilled through core,
epiphanies at times appear.

So silence we must understand
speaks ebb, lets waters contemplate.
In low tide, sifting sands expand
to ponder and extrapolate.

Laurie F. Grommett

Semi-Finalist of the "Poetry of the Ocean" Contest

Full Circle

Reaching out a helping hand
is an easy thing to do....

When giving help to those in need,
the gift comes back to you....

For, when you open up your heart
and help your fellow man....

The Love and Light come back to you,
right where it first began....

Sandy Jo Botello

Semi-Finalist of the "Selflessness-Why?" Contest

the midnight sail

Crack, a little sound from the mast
Reacting cordially to the touch of the monsoon
On her old wooden structure
A tender embrace he gives
Stretching wide the black canvas
Whispering tales of the brave
The once beautiful and strong
But now lay wrecked at sea bottom
Harboring souls of the dead
Captain Black and his crew
An old map of the sea
To the lost moving island
Resting the rulers of the sea
The great kings of pirates

Whoosh, gentle waves drifting
Rocking us rhythmically
A musical sensation it feels
Like a fine tune of a classical
Conducted live in the open sea
Trumpets, trombones and tubas
Violins, violas and harps
A symphonic sound for the traveling souls
And as the sea guardians work
Attending to Captain White in his cabin
I stand on the deck
Relishing the cold breeze
Watching the moon shift
On a midnight sail

Kayanja Ronald Edwin

Semi-Finalist of the "Poetry of the Ocean" Contest

She weeps in stars.

Mowers rattle in sprays
of green fountains
and barking dogs
echo in the
sacredness
of Sundays....

The sky
hanging in that
languid azure
of cloudless
benevolence.

See the horizontal stripes,
clipped into fragrant
shards
of ruthless garrottes.
Sparkling ligatures
of runoff
twisting and turning
through foolish
streams

Belly flopping from
the jetty
into bombs
of weed free
pest free
emerald desire
Where an abundance
bleeds
in phosphate

Splashing idly in an
empty sea
shining above a
star

littered sand

Trickling date
rape
of algal bloom
more vibrant
than
your perfect
scentless
rose

A weeping
river
cannot wash away
her defilement
as she pours
her grief into
the sea

As you mow the
sacred sands
on a rattling
Sunday
the timid dunes
and castles
watch the
waves

HUSHHH,
HUSHHH,
HUSHHHHH
soothes the lullaby,
as she tries to
scrub herself
clean
along a
distant shoreline....

and the ocean
weeps
in stars
upon the broken
coral sands

Ann Gilchrist

Semi-Finalist of the "Poetry of the Ocean" Contest

the shadow king

once just a canvas - ripped from the sands of time
a vast vapid absence that art has since defined

where winged flying fairy's - render from the sea
magic unicorns from the waves of waters free
a sacrificial offering to the evil shadow king
who sacrifices fairy's - as the oceans offering

the salty wet - buns already red eyes redder
watching as tidal roars - gets evermore wetter
pruned skin - sulfur stank - stings - wings sore - scorn
swings torn seams - tore more - waves crash - splash splatters
scatters pour - sweat stinks -beads drop – warm breze - thinks
pulls reacts - screams and retracts - still pulls - gets pulled back
howls hums vowels - lure - caught up in a constant tug of war
pushes pulling tugging - gore - yanks cranks - cracks snap
time stops - pauses - stands still silencing everything   -no more-
accept the shadow king [for he has won the war]

Joshua Joseph Bissot (PoetryDig.com)

Semi-Finalist of the "Poetry of the Ocean" Contest

Floating

Waves gently lapping upon the warm beach
in a universal . . . rhythmic heart beat,
instilling comfort and deep inner peace.

Time softens and it helps me to reach,
unison of breath flowing forth to greet
waves gently lapping upon the warm beach.

I float on this sea, and allow it to teach
me how to let go as the waves retreat,
instilling comfort and deep inner peace.

Worries wash away with the wave's soft speech
and a calmness bonds with this melody of sweet
waves gently lapping upon the warm beach.

Hopes once submerged, resurface now with each
round of ebb and flow making dreams replete,
instilling comfort and deep inner peace.

Now fortified, there's nothing that can breach
my desire to make my life complete.
Waves gently lapping upon the warm beach,
instilling comfort and deep inner peace.

Poetry Form: Villanelle

Debra M. Lalli

*Semi-Finalist of the "Poetry of the Ocean" Contest

~~*Ocean's Kiss*~~

In the surly dark depths of water,
Oceanic swells override the deep.
A surging momentum crests and falls,
but secrets are hidden low to keep.

Blue mirage of the rolling waves,
in the endless cerulean seascape,
teases to deceive a distance unknown,
where the undertow leaves no escape.

Working of tides, gnashing the shore,
in eruptions of white foamy spew,
create a blustery effect of salty mist,
that leaps from the briny brew.

Beckoning to birds who frequent,
who then put on quite a display.
Frolicking in breakers that crash,
to find morsels that come their way.

Calling of the gulls so seafaring,
they sing the melody of ocean lore.
Other creatures far beneath her shell,
dwell in solitude on the aquatic floor.

The azure blues of sea and sky,
part company at the end of day.
Where they bid adieu in scarlet ribbons,
of tangerine skies that meld into gray.

The ocean has kissed the sky,
and bid the earth,.. until nigh.

grandniem

Semi-Finalist of the "Poetry of the Ocean" Contest

Crescent Full Moon

The causeway
to South Padre
is thick

with a gloomy
rolling mist

Hiding
its glistening
green and blue bay

The hotels
Tower
like island mountains

Their peaks
above the morning fog

The silver
sliver
of the dying
crescent Moon
Pulls the tides
with all its might

The gulf's morning Sun
Fogged up

That crystal clear
dark night

The warm balcony
breeze

Holding promises
of hope
To the perfect

island day
Tough decisions
over bloody marys

we discuss

Do we swim in the gulf
or the bay

The beach was a buzz
amongst the flocking
tourist of white

Two chairs
our towels
a tan
and a cooler
full of delight
To see that deep dark blue
I must make part of my daily
morning sight

I walk into the tide
no wetsuit
Just my boogie
for this ride

" You were swimming amongst
a bunch of four foot sharks"

As I smile at the fisherman
with pride
No rip current
or undertow
It was on the top of the wave
I glide

As all the smiling

tourist stare

It was just my luck

to my ankles

My board shorts did slide

Cody Johnson

Semi-Finalist of the "Poetry of the Ocean" Contest

Her

selflessness
hides
strength
goodness
encourages
bridges
heart
cushions
failure
she
is
temper
she
is
fiery
she
is
woman

Chrissy Thompson

Semi-Finalist of the "Selflessness-Why?" Contest

The Mahasagar (In Hindi means, The Ocean)

Quietly I stood before you
With a heavy heart
I came to exhale the past and
Find a new future.

A blue body, such beauty!
Seeing you kissing the shore
Sometimes you rush
and give me a crush.

Just like asking me to face the risk
Your silence taught me to be brisk.
I know even your deepness
has many mysteries.

Blue Ocean
Your life may be like mine
With failures and trophies
Calm or still
Rough or smooth
rush and crush.

Now I learnt to swim
In ocean of life
Just i have to dive in
take the risk to
Cross the stormy winds,
Tough tides and deeper currents.

To redefine my treasure
Nothing but a beautiful Life

Kiruthika Karthik

Semi-Finalist of the "Poetry of the Ocean" Contest

Jun 26, 2016

Peaceful Coexistence

Pacific blue.
Clandestine cove
woven..in..waves
of eternal mind.

Crashing shore
breaking..the..hold
of insecurities.

Sit and watch,
reminiscing.
How..many..lives
will be led?

Which..serendipitous..sands
the most cherished?
Will heaven involve
a choice or will the choice
itself..be..hell?

Has..my..life
been an allegory
for hope
or
for anomie?

The rainbows held
in the salty spray
spring..geysers..of
recurring
smiles..smiles..smiles.

Hope,
like waves
cannot..be..grasped
and held.
Only ridden

if..well..timed.

Therein lies
the fascination
of..the..mid-line.
The open space
between
exhilaration and sleep,
fireworks..and..nightmares.

Composing muses
and being composed
become..twinned..zygotes
that grow
in..warm..tide pools
gazing prematurely
at life's verbiage
from underneath
orange..red..eyelids.

Iff Ur Abs

*Semi-Finalist of the "Poetry of the Ocean" Contest

The Ballad of a Brave Man

Excerpt from a letter written by a young New Zealand boy to his
sweetheart during WW1
"The sounds of dying men are soft
Their voices hushed with fear,
They speak of how they cannot wait
To see their mothers dear.

'Oh Mother, Mother,' the refrain,
Their dying crowds my ears
On foreign soils, so far from home
All die at Chunuk Bair."

They drafted him against his will
And armed him to the hilt,
Then held him behind prison gates
With others of his ilk.

To take up arms, he told them nay,
And never would retract
His faith that God Almighty held,
All life as sacrosanct.

Refrain
He was a brave man, a brave man
His manner light not loud
And none would ever doubt again,
He made his country proud.

They threatened death and forfeiture
Stitched red cross on his arm
And hauled him off to war in chains
To pluck our boys from harm.

The path he walked was not his choice
And therein lay some shame
But from that day he pledged his faith,
He'd walk it just the same.

He dodged the shells, he ducked the shot
He'd never make them wait
When "Stretcher Bearer" came the call,
He did not hesitate.

How many times he crept behind
The enemy that day,
To drag the dead and dying home
No one can truly say.

But when the heat of battle eased
And he could not be found
They looked out over no man's land
And saw his corpse earth bound.

Refrain

Bev Pollard

*Semi-Finalist of the "Selflessness-Why?" Contest

Measure of a Man

How do you define a man?
By his bravery?
By how fiercely his lionheart beats,
Defiant in facing danger?
Does his courage powerfully course
Through each vein?
Is that what makes a man?

Is he a fearless warrior?
A daring and audacious hero?
If these are measures of a man,
I find myself wondering
If we will ever meet one.
No, this is nothing but false bravado.
But You have shown us what a true man is.

He is brave!
He looks into fear and can weep,
Even tears of blood.
But He endures.
He humbly approaches danger.
He only acts with love.
Even when faced with death,

With being beaten and ripped raw,
He doesn't look away.
Not out of ferocity or acrimony,
But love and a quiet mind.
He does not trust in His own strength,
But Yours!
He is willing to throw Himself into the chasm,

Knowing He will be engulfed.
A real man doesn't fight for what he believes in,
But lives and dies for it.
He knows that You are our fortress.
That through Your lovingkindness,

We do not end.
We only begin again.

Stephen Peake

Semi-Finalist of the "Selflessness-Why?" Contest

Not bad

You can get it frozen
or fresh from the oven
With a myriad of toppings
makes some a glutton

Can be round or square
deep dish or thin
White sauce or red
possibilities never end

Eat with caution though
Pizza mouth really burns
scalding the palat
A hot lesson learned

There's an old saying
It's simply not complex

Even when pizzas bad

It's still desired
just like sex

WholeHeart aka Tom Harmon

Semi-finalist of the "Pizza, Pizza!!" Contest

Two Legged Mammals Molest You

Like Lamebrains.

The Man Begs Pardon Of Earth

The Man Begs Pardon Of Earth
Oceans-attired and endowed with the
bosoms of vast high mountains
with multitudes of flora and fauna
with rivers lakes and wild fountains.

How you dispense the light, air
and water free, amazed are accountants.
What we hear are just names
ecological campaigns as if said as rants.

Oceans-attired and endowed with the
bosoms of vast high mountains.
with multitudes of flora and fauna
with rivers lakes and wild fountains.

Pardon me O, mother as the most
despicable being, I trample you.
No other sources of livelihood I have
still I conspire, dismantle you.

Like O-lan* of "Good Earth", killing her
female kiddy, I strangle you.
Empty udders on machines reclaim land
by ill- means like egg, I scramble you.

The two-legged mammals molest you
ceaselessly like lamebrains.
Oceans-attired and endowed with
the bosoms of vast mountains
with multitudes of flora and fauna
with rivers lakes, wild fountains.

Man's Prayer

May the heavens stay in peace may the earth stay at ease.
May there be no sickness, no grief, may there be no disease.
May the herbs plants and animals enjoy eternal bliss and peace.

May all enjoy fortune and health, may all be on a century- lease.
May O, Lord thy grace embrace me too, may I too dwell in peace.
May we not make fun, ridicule dwarf dart or black, may we not
tease.

The Truth Ultimate

Look at skies, the ethereal, it is complete it is whole,
look at the Universe, it's integral, abundant and whole.
The whole arises from and is manifested by the whole.
If you attempt to take away ever the whole from whole.
What goes gets replenished soon remnant is still whole!

Abhilaaj

Semi-Finalist of the "Kogi Mama" Contest

A Name Already Known

We keep on naming the babies
all the names
we already know
and nothing happens.

Everything circles around,
drifting together,
swimming apart,
combined and remixed
into hip hop parades crawling from
the black and white past
into the color that exploded
from Hiroshima's song demanding
a bended knee from Apollo,
illuminating
the quadrilateral
digest inside
the platonic dialogue
climbing the fire escape
towards Mars.

And Blake is still
making the divine image
out of the human form
as if we are martyrs
all burning together
with a single yawn
waiting to sleep together
in the orgy between the sky.

We dream
and have no glory,
waiting for the next
reincarnation
where we will not remember
as we wake again

to a new light of dawn
with a name already known.

Robert Szankowski

*Semi-Finalist of the "Kogi Mama" Contest

Oceans Emotions

An infinite horizon
Where the sky
Embraces the ocean
Passionate waves
Rushing with deep
Silver emotions
To tenderly touch
The shores with love
Transparent clouds
Floating with golden wings
Like heavenly angels
The sun shyly diving
Into the blue water
Caressing the night
In a majestic scene
Imagery of serene beauty
A spiritual trance
Pure peaceful intimacy
Created by The Divine
As evidence to the unity
Of planetary motion

Essama Chiba

*Semi-Finalist of the "Poetry of the Ocean" Contest

Land of toys

Fellow compatriots,
I've got a super vision
to build this jungle nation.
I'm the god of politics
not a quark magician.

I remain your motivation,
take, hid to my constitution.
If you disjoin, bury your
craves within your ribs,
sew your lips to your notions,
glide and explore confusion.

Freewill's a free kill-nut...
To every man I ride on,
enjoy this rebellious dominion,
be imperious and heroic
for this is a nation of toys...
These lethal toys protect
in the quest to vanquish
whom you deem fit
to benefit some peanuts

You all are judges bestowed
to array your suspects in
your hidden chambers.
More so, to gift verdicts
like freebies of bouquet
to the puny and celebrate
their executions in an
open banquet, all in one,
as quickly as an instant.

You may as well romance
your skull with the silver
ornament and swallow
its tablets to cure all pains

and land you in a paradise
to lie on a rose-full bed
in a happy forever after
on empty dreams and trills.

This day I present to you
a golden anarchy; we are
the gods of life and death;
we take away the joy
of mothers, the pride
of fathers and beloved.

The benefactors of tears
and super DJs remixing
the sounds of fireworks
and force our infants to our
night clubs, so that they may
return no more as they float
on their own pool of red sea,
while sailing to an oblivious
destination in their undesired
and everlasting odysseys.

But, we hire Pitbulls
for personal guards,
send our pretty chihuahuas
to carry upon themselves
sophisticated, over-weight
rifles so they may become
super-duper mini-heroes
which we forbid in ourselves.

Recent statistics show
how greatly we have soared
successfully in the quest to quell
our kindred for protection;
in fact it has overwhelmed us
such that we celebrate tears
which erode our fertile land,

giving pale flowers to the bereaved.
More flowers are reserved
in our central flower banks
and a profusion of handkerchiefs,
everyone is eligible, no age
restrictions nor are there
sanity tests, even psychopaths
and our fellas by minus two DNA!
Come one, come all, as we make
this land of toys fun by availing
your license to slaughter
and butcher one another.

Destiny Izehi
Editor: Ron

Semi-Finalist of the "Kogi Mama" Contest

Save a couple of slices

Thin bread baked till crisp across,
draped in scarlet pizza sauce,
sprinkled with mince and mushroom,
olives and onions abloom,
garnished with hot peppers green,
bits of garlic in between,
crowned with warm coveted cheese.

crimsondew / Firdous Arjumand

Semi-finalist of the "Pizza, Pizza!!" Contest

The Oracle

We rip her of her dignity and barren is her womb,
"Too late she cries, my tears are dry and now we all face doom.
I begged for you to treat me with a tender, caring touch,
but now what's left of me is really nothing very much."

We've raked the goodness from her ground and sprayed the toxins
out,
then left the residues to burn without a thought or doubt.
The rain then comes and washes them into the gleaming streams,
without a care of restoration, on to other schemes.

The stream will flow as it must do into the mighty sea,
and takes the poisons with it killing creatures harmony.
The balance shifts and suddenly the perils are immense,
whilst people start debating, seems without much common sense.

And on we go discovering the miracles she holds,
as money making plans a-plenty suddenly unfolds.
Those thoughts of the effect we'll have upon her symmetry,
all seem to go unheeded with a lost identity.

But then her anger starts to shout as she is fighting back,
against what was our willful pride that dragged her way off track.
We made her air polluted and she's spewing great disease,
with atmosphere that's heating up in sickening degrees.

The native, Hollow Horn Bear, heard her pleas so long ago,
and with his words he tried to tell us not to let her go.
And maybe now we're listening to what he did foretell,
but are our choices changing and can earth again be well?

-JR-

Semi-Finalist of the "Kogi Mama" Contest

After the apocalypse has begun...

I am a deserted cabin left by a lonesome woodcutter,
He had to chop trees for earning his bread and butter.

He'd no one staying with him, so he used to talk to me,
We chatted after he did his work, getting some time free.

Before sleeping, he often felt gloomy about his own life,
His parents had left him an orphan, he never had a wife.

He felt that I were a place to sleep but not his real home,
Since he was a child, for earning his living, he'd to roam.

I listened to him with patience whatever he liked to say,
But one day I asked him can I speak my mind, if I may.

He smiled at my request and said he was ready to hear,
He wanted to know my take, as his stint's end was near.

I said he never made a home, but roamed cutting wood,
Using it to make cabins, in which no one stayed for good.

But the green forests and shady trees lining Mother Earth,
Which men destroy for petty gains, have a priceless worth.

To make houses and buildings, they're eroding our planet,
Since a tree lost its life for making me, may I humbly solicit.

For temporary shelters, don't forget your permanent abode,
With most of the greenery denuded, you must stop to erode.

Or your future generations will have to find a home in space,
When with global warming, Earth will become a hostile place.

My appeal touched his heart so much, he left his job for good,
He promised me that he would do anything but never cut wood.

Now in this jungle, I stand wondering if my words inspired him,
Why don't the learned folks understand that their future is grim.

If they don't do for preserving environment what should be done,
There will be a point of no return after the apocalypse has begun!

Dr. Asghar Nazeer

*Semi-Finalist of the "Kogi Mama" Contest

Spellbound

The sky had always beckoned me
with blue as far as I could see,
and clouds of castles, mountains, beasts—
a vast expanse from west to east.
It made me wonder as I'd gaze
from fields below on summer days;
how far away could heaven be?
And then one day I saw the sea.

Its cresting waves and heaving swells
pulled in to shore a thousand shells
which told the story of the deep.
I knew that day that I would keep
the majesty of surf and spray
within me 'til my dying day,
that salty air would scent my mind,
whatever wonders I might find,
and in my sleep the screeching gull
would echo through my dreaming lull.
The sky had always called to me—
and then there was the sea...

Katharine L. Sparrow

*Semi-Finalist of the "Poetry of the Ocean" Contest

Breaking Ground (Ottava Rima)

Industrial improvements built their bed,
then hand-to-mouth existence up and flown.
It loomed with greying smokestacks overhead,
polluting street conditions to bare bone.
The factories made jobs for folks and fed
their families and set an urban tone.

Contaminating cancers grew a girth
while Bills of Rights stood printing out their worth.

A blinding alley birthed in cobblestones,
each block of brick gave man a fighting chance.
Removal of a ruling reign of thrones
bred manufactured means to ford advance.
The betterment of some made others clones,
while banks grew hungry belly for finance.

With pockets full of cash to pay the bills,
we bought and sold from company owned mills.

Consumption of resources cost a price
when assets turn to liability
as investment becomes a sacrifice.
Who absorbs the burden, culpability
on streets all festered with a crowd of mice.
Production labeled past reality.

We dealt in darkness, courted prostitution.
The day demands a light of restitution.

Laurie F. Grommett

Semi-Finalist of the "Kogi Mama" Contest

sliced tomatoes - haiku

sliced tomatoes
on a cheesy flat-bread
olive garden

RiAnne Hawley

Semi-Finalist of the "Pizza, a haiku" Contest

Haiku #495 (thin crust)

thin crust
with meat and cheese
aha!!! goldfish

James W. McRight Jr.

Semi-Finalist of the "Pizza, a haiku" Contest

mozzarella Bliss

mozzarella bliss
with sizzling pepperoni
diners salivate

Donald G. Zielinski

Semi-Finalist of the "Pizza, a haiku" Contest

Society

I am what you made me
All that I have is all that you gave me
Heart broken promises and
tear soaked hope
Oh' please let me smile again!

Society
The illusionist
The drunken revolutionist
The owner of slaves
Oh' please let me trust again!

Society
I just couldn't be like you
Your lies I could see through
Fairy-tales at dusk and
murder at dawn
Oh' please let me believe again!

Society
Unapologetic
Unsympathetic
Your blood soaked truth synthetic
Oh' please let me roam the woods again!

Society
I studied very hard
and memorized your secrets
but you leave me with this bleakness
the curves of your hips were my weakness
and the touch of your lips left me sleepless
Oh' please let me dream again!

Society
Why did your "liberation" escape me?
Why did your freedom evade me?

Why did you have to betray me?
Oh' please let me love again!

Mark Moir

*Semi-Finalist of the "Kogi Mama" Contest

golden shoes & diamonds too

I lost my way, far away from home.
My shoes I made from gold I never owned.
Still I walked like the righteous man, alone?
All alone in shoes with no soles.
The bottoms of my feet just blood and bone.

And where have I gone?
To some carnival of shame~
where fires burned away every letter of my name.
I look back and all I can see are bloodied footprints
upon the ruination of every thing that ever spoke of me.
--
My diamonds in hand, within a pill bottle they rattle.
Marching away towards nothing that matters.
I shine and I glitter,
all the way to Hell,
where my end will be bitter,
under this spell.

iKael

*Semi-Finalist of the "Kogi Mama" Contest

Why on Earth

the deceit
on our grandchildren
fabricated ways of
thinking it's easier if we pretend
blind

smoke on the horizon
smells bitter, far from sweet

levels of carbon dioxide 1969 in atmosphere 330ppm
standard of living by gross world product 12 000 billion dollars
population 3, 616, 108, 749 leaves 3 318 dollars per capita

child and the candy char, only given one
char and the child with adult gone out of the building

instead of hitting
we slaughter our children

how on Earth

lake can vanish in the mind of a child
and in the eyes closed by adult
bubble bath bay no child would ever go
no adult has seen
stings the stink of chemicals
trees awe and weep
waters move in shivering agony

level of carbon dioxide 1989 in atmosphere 358ppm
as man made march of money goes on
standard of living by gross world product 26 500 billion dollars
population 5, 230, 452, 409 leaves 5 066 dollars per capita

the obesity of greed
once considered a cardinal sin(s)
where to put the stuff we buy and buy and

buy...and have to buy a bigger house

impatience of a child seem infectious to adults
building up money based careers upon the
principalities of lust for more

land of ice is land of ice
never change, the glaciers, only melt
in children's mind
dreamful role plays of queens of ice
and behind back
turned by
adults

car tends to provide you with overwhelming heat when
one turns off air conditioning on sunny day
when windows are closed -
this planet is a car

how on Earth

is it so hard to see even if eyes closed
feel the heat
in the car

level of carbon dioxide 2009 in the atmosphere 390ppm
lot is only a lot in comparison to what
we had, greed is always more and
plenty will turn into too few
standard of living by gross world product 58 500 billion dollars
population 6, 834, 721, 933 leaves
8 559 dollars per capita

deserts are flooding, expansionists
forests are falling, down
and burning
erosion, hurricanes, massive raining, too hot, too cold, typhoons,
flooding, snow not falling, ice is melting, cities polluted,
heatwaves, cars, coal plants, unnecessary things we buy and buy

and buy and throw away, non-recycling behavior, deeds we do in
everyday life, the politicians we elect, shame on else   not, shame
on ourselves, country by city by block by house by people, it is the
individual choice we make every day

normally when one hears sirens
the help is on its way

past times ruined land saw rats
leaving the sinking ship
rats find there way
to survive any maze
except
the caged one

even a child can understand sirens
mean trouble and
need to fulfill the aid forsooth

adults are touching the air
between the bars

even blind man can feel them
the cold

amounts of carbon dioxide in future rises, more people inhabit
the still beautiful planet, we'll get richer the more and richer some
more
the standard of living
not by dollars
as we toss the place in flames and
tell the sirens to take it easy
?

how on Earth

V.S. Paavolainen

Semi-Finalist of the "Kogi Mama" Contest

Continuance

I

there are times
I feel I'm drowning
in the midst of chaos

fear and agony seize
my core existence
and desolation threatens

devouring the depths
of my embodiment

it is in these times
you are nearest to me

every inhalation
renewing life

desperately I cleave
endless devotion onto you

for only through you
can life's aspirations
ever be replenished

II

and though darkness
approaches

fear not

for beauty lies there in

withal

even as we bathe
in tears of injustice
filth and sorrow

this inescapable nemesis
we will conquer
and over throw

hold fast onto destiny
fortuity is by our side

triumphing
over ruination

III

every teardrop
surrendered

will be a prescription
for misfortune's architect

carrying eternal death

execute anathema's
abomination upon
this phantom wraith

devour and paint him
into anonymity

from manifestation

giving adversary
what is due

IV

holdfast

till day light
shines upon us

once again

the tender moments
and memories
we will reminisce

celebrating
the brevity of life

allowing love to embrace
a birthplace for two hearts

once more

two transient vessels
in search of an everlasting
cosmos

Chrysanthy Pappas

*Semi-Finalist of the "Kogi Mama" Contest

Haiku.6

rustic wood-fired dough
served with pizzaz
cheesy

Shobha S Rao

*Semi-Finalist of the "Pizza, a haiku" Contest

shocked cries

shocked cries on
pizza for breakfast
why not

Mary Lou Healy

Semi-Finalist of the "Pizza, a haiku" Contest

haiku (three toppings)

three toppings
on cheesy crust
tomato allergy

Laurie F. Grommett

Semi-Finalist of the "Pizza, a haiku" Contest

pizza 'ku

red sunset~
tomato, cheese, sausage
deep dish delight

Dennis L. White

Semi-Finalist of the "Pizza, a haiku" Contest

Pizza

Melting slowly under the grill
A work of art is slowly coming to perfection
Grated mozzarella meets parmesan
Nuzzled tween, Sicilian ham and Neapolitan tomatoes
In places, the rich red sauce shows through
For this is a work of art
It was formed in the mind of a master craftsman
Crafted by his learned apprentices...And finished with
Oregano picked fresh from the garden.

Brian F Kirkham aka InkdropK

Semi-finalist of the "Pizza, Pizza!!" Contest

Cowabunga

Yellow triangles bubbling with love,
gondolas of pepperoni floating,
drifting across oceans of red sauce.

Delivered in dirty boxes soak through with grease,
each slice pulling at webs of cheese.

Crispy, Gooey, Spicy, sometimes Sweet,
every bite a love affair to be devoured by the soul.

Sam Irvin

Semi-finalist of the "Pizza, Pizza!!" Contest

And Tomorrow Will Surely Come

One image remains
as the world is torn asunder
in racist disparagement

so much easier to denigrate another
to enable me,
to bolster pyrite confidence
in defects I shelve beneath cold shadows
than to accept another has equal
or superior, ability

it is, after all, my perception
of the world that deserves recognition
and while I strain to carry the weight
of my grandeur with lacklustre poise
I have at least, usurped the dignity
of lesser beings

and I command attention
like Canute, my plastic throne
entitles me to direct the incoming tides
to obey authority not yet granted
nor respected
by my fellow citizens

I revel in the carnage of my passions
leaving a footprint of dominance
in a wake filled with mire
as I feed my hunger at the expense
of my brother's aspirations

ah, but one image remains…
a silhouette wearing the jester's crown
and though my smile is borrowed
from a cereal box
I will ever deny ownership of that effigy
suspended

from a hangman's noose
while gossips gather in phalanxes of hope
to hail the new dawn
of tolerance

Alf Collier

Semi-finalist of the "One Today" Contest

Olives

They put olives on my pizza, I don't like them
now my whole lunch is ruined don't you see
for I never learned the knack
of sending products back
when they don't match with what they ought to be

So I'll eat around the ghastly green invaders
I'm somewhat picky I have to confess
and at the waitresses appeal
of 'did you enjoy your meal?'
being British I will smile and answer yes

But my plate will give the lie to that assertion
the evidence is plain for all to see
for it looks like a disaster
and the mess that remains after
an explosion in a pizza factory

Chris the Rhymer / Chris Daws

Semi-finalist of the "Pizza, Pizza!!" Contest

Earth Shadows

Can we distinguish darkness from the shadows,
in this rhythmic dance of Mother Earth...?
From the misty meadows, to mighty mountains,
where nature silently reclaims her birth...

There behind the shadows, looking so forlorn,
in windswept darkness, stood my spirit guide...
Blaming not, this quiet essence from nature,
yet standing so solemn, still, by my side...

"Can she but heal herself", my spirit asked me,
"Without a seed, can a little flower grow...?
Does the gentle rain upon the mighty mountains,
create rivers un-dammed, and left to flow"...?

In the cloudy blue of a warm summer's day,
the magical rhythm of all nature sings...
The babbling brooks recall earth's stories,
as the meadowlarks again take to wing...

"Only our dead can be forgiven", he whispers,
fading again in shadows, he so harshly sigh's...
Blaming not, this quiet essence of nature,
in shame, I slowly hang my head and cry...!

We are walking on the bones of our ancestors.
Through the atmosphere, ground, and water.
Whether it's bone and flesh or ashes, the aspect
of our ancestors is dispersed into this land. We
owe it to them to protect Mother Earth. Native
American belief

Melody Hamby Goss

Semi-Finalist of the "Kogi Mama" Contest

Poetry Hand Selected

For Excellence

The Road Not Taken

Two roads diverged in a yellow wood,
And sorry I could not travel both
And be one traveler, long I stood
And looked down one as far as I could
To where it bent in the undergrowth;

Then took the other, as just as fair,
And having perhaps the better claim,
Because it was grassy and wanted wear;
Though as for that the passing there
Had worn them really about the same,

And both that morning equally lay
In leaves no step had trodden black.
Oh, I kept the first for another day!
Yet knowing how way leads on to way,
I doubted if I should ever come back.

I shall be telling this with a sigh
Somewhere ages and ages hence:
Two roads diverged in a wood, and I—
I took the one less traveled by,
And that has made all the difference.

Robert Frost

A Masterpiece

All alone in the field,
No one to listen to her sing
She was happy but she wasn't!
Even the author knew nothing.
He knew her song was a melancholy strain
which made even the passers by stop to hear.

In school times
My memories hold the poem lines
Read this first, second and third time
Finally memorized the whole one
Just for getting marks.

The day came
When I, too, became a poet
It made me feel and enjoy poems.
That's the time I turned over the pages of my old books
It took me to some poems like, The Road not Taken, Paper Boats,
The Solitary Reaper, Daffodils, Lucy Gray so on
From the core of my heart
I was able to enjoy and feel and
I started loving those...

A poet is who writes from the depths of his heart
Who make others
Enjoy his happiness,
Feel his loveliness,
Cry for his sadness,
Then, even his silence speaks

Kiruthika Karthik

Another September ...

Oh, Autumn trees, the flutes, the flutes are sighing
Down country lanes, and by the mountain brook;
The Summer's gone; your leafy show is dying;
It's you and you must fall and I but look.

Yet you'll return when Spring comes in the meadows
Or when the Summer blush lies on you bright;
And I'll be here in blue skies or in shadows--
Oh, Autumn trees! This moment loves your sight.

And if I come when all the leaves are flying;
And if I die, as die I well could do,
You'll cover where the gravestone will be lying
And color there, to touch with mourning dew.

And I shall know, though soft you lie above me;
And all my dreams with warmth of brown and red
Shall shelter me from cold blasts in each tree
Where there, in peace, that moment's in my head.

Oh, Autumn trees, the flutes, the flutes are sighing
Down country lanes, and by the mountain brook;
The summer's gone; your leafy show is dying;
It's you and you must fall and I but look.

Yet you'll return when Spring comes in the meadows
Or when the Summer blush lies on you bright;
And I'll be here in blue skies or in shadows--
Oh, Autumn trees! This moment loves your sight,

Where there, in peace, I lie there, tombstone dead;
For I have come when all the leaves are flying;
Till then, my dreams are warm with earthy red.
Oh, autumn trees, the flutes, the flutes are sighing.

Ron Wiseman

keep the rain

I'm glad
the sun came out,
but I was just getting used
to the sweet melancholy

of the rain.

Joe Slotnick

Your Muse

And she your muse now entertains,
Surrounded by the music, reigns,
And in amazement do you stare,
A fact that goes not unaware;
Enthralled you must appreciate,
Such perfect form commensurate
With that of an immortal God,
Upon whose path you faithful trod;
She smiles and condescends to read,
You beg forgiveness, nay you plead,
No reason for she nods assent,
An affirmation, her consent
To write again, inspired once more,
By she whom you respect, adore.

Alistair Muir

The Secret of a Thing

He was no April Fool
though born on that day
so I had to play.

Every year the same:
pebbles in his shoes
salt in his morning coffee.

You bitch! with a smile on his face,
pretending to be surprised:

we walked in dew
talked in colors
lied down under the stars
watched snow pass evening streetlights through the window

And the ocean has not been so quiet for a long while.

Diane Gwynne Allen

Precision

Sunlight steps out of
a grey mantle of raindrops;
she contemplates bees hopping
in Fibonacci spirals,
tiny physicists teaching Einstein
precision.

Deb Blondell-Pitt

Through Children's Eyes

I watched you as you painted stars
in seas of indecision,
a child of innocence you painted
with picture perfect vision.

You saw the world through eyes of hope
where all was brilliant light,
the moon and stars arrayed to cast
the shadows from the night.

If only all of us could see a picture
as bright and crystal clear,
pain would be a thing of the past,
our sorrows disappear

And so I pray tonight to see the world
through children's eyes,
where all is calm, and peace abounds
not fear and war and lies.

Michele Wass

Vision Power

Ship anchored in surrender
Goodness grounded in faith
Harmonious nature nurtured
Beauty bends to Grace divine
Verse performs in great wisdom
Universal art in musical rhyme
Greatness born of potential
Poetic vision-

Andrea Owens

Flute Music

It was soft wood,
tender like the notes traveling
through cedar forests
where woodpeckers
hollowed holes in branches
and wind played dulcet tones
along the Mississippi.

It was here, her lips
held him captive, as he sat
cross-legged under tender
boughs, her boughs stirring
as she carried melodies
soft from the cedar, touching
each note . . . warbling octaves
from her breath in whispered
moments.

Diane Gwynne Allen

November Twilight

Lowering skies with a wintery breeze,
And the trees' naked branches sway;
With silent feet on the sodden leaves
I wander at close of day.
All the world is gray, and the birds have gone,
And the flowers lie wrapped in sleep,
Where the lengthening shadows creep.

Bethany S. Wright

The Measure of a Man

"The world is a fine place and worth the fighting for

and I hate very much to leave it." Earnest Hemingway

How do we tell the measure of a man?
By his size? By his stamina? By his age?

They teased him for being
old and without luck,
but from behind
they saw his muscular back
his strong neck
and his powerful arms.

Do we tell the measure of a man
by his determination and resilience?

I am the man who arm-wrestled,

and won the champion from Casablanca:
elbows down, hands grasped, faces tense.
For two days, and one night we struggled.
I am DiMaggio, playing ball in pain.
I am the lions on the African beach.
I am King of the jungle
I am
a master fisherman.

The blue sea shown in the old man's eyes, as
he seized the rope, and saw the Marlin's
head, shining purple under the bright sun.
Jump again fish, show me your might.
Show me who you really are. When
we're done, you will be mine.

The sound of clicking jaws,
kept beat with the current,
as it moved home.
The battle of endurance to the fullest,
a struggle to the end,
and the perilous journey's boon: a skeleton.

How do we tell the measure of a man?

Diane Gwynne Allen

Pleiades

What is a year?
Merely a wisp of smoke,
the single beat of a moth's wing,
from where the stars converge on infinity.

Eons before the earth burst forth in fruit and frond,
they wheeled above
like colossal motes of dust in a shaft of moonlight,
calling forth the spark of life from nothingness.

Now, in that blink of time
that begins the turn of the seasons,
they shine—
a churning brew of startling beauty
that takes the breath away—
captured in awed astonishment
by eternity.

Katharine L. Sparrow

torn paper

I was
a paper doll
inside a broken
dark box

disheveled,
tattered,
alone

no one wants
to play with
a damaged
paper doll

you came along,
opened my box,
picked me up

no one had picked
me up
in such a long
long time,
I feared
I would crumble

my smile crooked
my contacts missing

you seemed
not to notice,
found a beautiful
pink gown,
dressed me,
called me princess

''princess?'

I asked,
you smiled
read my mind
and whispered,

'the best thing
in life is
to hold another,'

you did just that-

we began-

you saw only
my perfections,
never tried
to fix me,
you just stayed

and stayed
until I knew
I was not tattered

I realize
all break,
sometime

my inside scars
began to fade,
you stayed

everything began
to begin anew
****

dark stitches
that fastened
my coat
now glitter

you are near

and I—
never again
will know
darkness

crumbs.of.sorts.

Firefly

My eyes adjusted to the black starless sky

meandering,

into the night.

Searching eagerly for a firefly
to assist me in my sight,

till
morning greets the Sun in flight.

Essama Chiba

time does not always change history

sometimes the black stays

with shades lost -
it's been so long

yet,
you have not changed

since my last poem,
for you

i was,
writing to draw out the light,
from your shade-less heart,

which
too, never changed shape.

with shades lost,
your same shape
and my time -

i did wait

Alison Emery

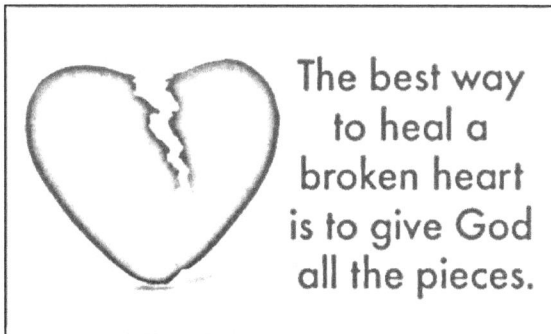

The best way
to heal a
broken heart
is to give God
all the pieces.

CutestPage.com

Avante-garde Jazz Malarkey

Piano cat plays pitter pat
and keys the board
of sharps
and flats.

A "catcophony" rat-a-tat,
his paws split out
and then
he scats.

He skips the scales from do to ti
in jazzy Joplin
ragtime
spree.

No twinkle toe agility,
he hunts and pecks
one pounce
a flee!

Laurie F. Grommett

Stripped Bare

I haven't got a thing to write about
so I will play Mah-Jong while counting geese,
or maybe scream and jump or even shout
and you can say ' This is a masterpiece'
My muse is in Barbados for week;
she said that I could come but I said no;
perhaps I'll give the second line a tweak
as geese are out of season, don't you know.
You said I could write anything I want,
you did, oh yes you did, well this is it,
I even used a rather fancy font
and fudged a bit so that the words would fit.
I know I won't win gold but I don't care,
but you can read it in your underwear.

Barry Hopkins

Sonnet

'Tis a sonnet with a complicated twist
using words that people very seldom see,
like abacinate, chirotonsor and schist
and petrichor and fiddle-diddle - dee.
They confuse because they positively can
leaving readers in a xylopolic tizz,
they are sometimes used in China or Japan
be they hers or be they sometimes known as his.
Though this sonnet really makes no sense at all
it is all I have to offer, my oh my;
I have written it in sciapodous scrawl
and I will do till the moment that I die.
Fare-thee-well, I've really had about enough
with this capernoited, estrapade and stuff.

Barry Hopkins

Nostalgic Remembrance

Bottom land so rich with life, in summers swell.
Staggered trees, dot meadow of emerald green.
Quaint summer cottages border this field
along lazy deep water creek.

A steady stream, of the station waggoned middle class
filters into, this child's realm of enchantment.
Shades drawn, dust covers are lifted,
giving flight to pixie dusted bunnies
sparkling in the light of celebrated freedom.

Mom spreads red and white checkered table-cloth
slowly floating down to cover
a weather worn picnic table.

Splashing sounds of delight carry back to the cottage.
The children have found the "Tarzan" swing
tied to a long overhanging branch
of this perfect old red oak,
that stretches far enough over the water.

Dad breaks out the charcoal,
lighter fluid at the ready.
He breaths in the scent of petroleum
and empties the can in the grille.

Match struck, eyebrows singed, face blackened.
For Dad, this tactile ritual, makes the holiday real.

Mom silently laughs as she rolls her eyes remembering
"It's funny how some things never change"
"Yes I'm still married to a child"

Water logged, sun burnt and exhausted
The scent of barbequed chicken and hot dogs
is carried on a gentle summer breeze,
reminding the children's empty stomachs

that it's time, to come home and re-fuel.

Bug lamps lit, to keep mosquitoes at bay
they yawn contentment,
with the bliss of full bellies.
Funny how there's always room
for a sweet wedge of watermelon.

Evening descends upon the meadow.
As enchantment awakens, the fireflies dance,
to a chorus of singing crickets.

Mom and Dad carry the little ones
to their cots in the summer cottage.

Smiling they head for the screen house
and the stars that blanket the night.

William J. Reed IV

It matters not

it matters not the cloths you wear
or how you dress or style your hair
yes fancy cars will take you far
don't live too fast and slight the stars
be gentle when you cross your foe
for it is he that failed to grow
walk steady with your head held high
seek sunsets when you can
follow your heart in ways of love
and you shall be a man.

Maria Oday

forte

pigment's
palette
etched a passage

painted white
with hues
of vesper's song

softly roping braille

and writing
stamps unseen
upon the latitude of my cross

a journey breathed
astride old grey

destined for returns
echoed back to you

until then
i rest

within the forte
of solitude

while silence reigns
as comforter

a courteous old friend

until then
the eminence
of peace resounds

Chrysanthy Pappas

Firefly

My eyes adjusted to the black starless sky

meandering,

into the night.

Searching eagerly for a firefly
to assist me in my sight,

till
morning greets the Sun in flight.

Maria Oday

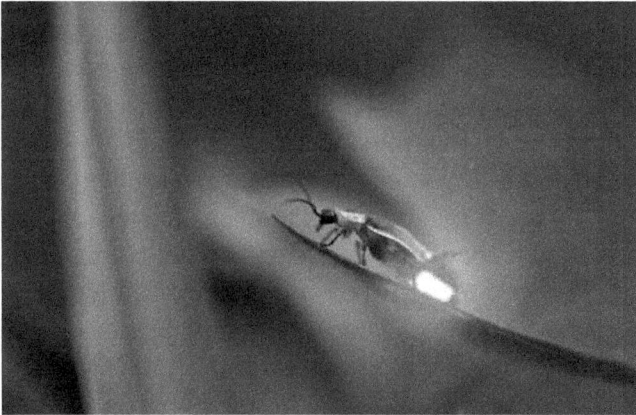

Good Shepherd Show...

Good Shepherd show the honest way
where we'll not from your pastures stray;
ensure in truth-sown fields we'll share
a moral compass ever there.

Ron Wiseman

The Political Campaign of 'Larry the Liar'

When 'Larry the liar' began his campaign
An omen occurred, which was four days of rain.
So all his supporters, with heads cocked would strain
To try and hear 'Larry the liar' explain ...
With thoughts fairly random that popped in his brain,
With words often vulgar and sometimes profane,
How he'd rearrange our whole orbital plane,
And make sure the Earth would get moving again.

"Has it stopped?" Someone asked? Larry flashed them a smile,
"The Earth's locked in place now for quite a long while
And what's more" he bellowed, "Is tragically true,
My opponent's begun to stop Earth's spinning, too!
And what happens then? If my sources are right
The world will be locked in perpetual night!
Then all of your lives will be too tough to save
As thousands of dinosaurs rise from the grave!"

His short, stout opponent was Dip Barleywine
Who stepped to his mic and said, "Everything's fine.
It's blather, and bother, tempest in a teacup,
For 'Larry the liar' has made the whole thing up."
"Are we really safe?" a reporter asked Dip,
"Well, no. You're not safe from his rogue salesmanship.
But as for Earth's spinning and orbital plane
It's fine, you can tell by the Moon's wax and wane."

"DON'T LISTEN TO HIM FOR HE'S EVIL CLEAR
THROUGH!"
Said 'Larry the liar' his face turning blue.
"HE'S ALWAYS DISHONEST, HE'LL SWINDLE YOU ALL
HOW COULD ANYONE TRUST A MAN ONLY THIS TALL?"
But, Dip Barleywine smiled, then danced round and round
And said, "I'm tall enough so my feet reach the ground.
I know that he's lying and I'll tell you why,
From the tides on the beach and the stars in the sky.

If we had stopped flat on the orbital plane,

Each night stars would be in the same place again.
But they move with the seasons and that's how I know
That Larry the liar has stooped very low.

His other bold lie, that the world has stopped spinning"
(At this point Dip Brandeywine couldn't stop grinning)
"Is disproven down where they keep science things
You can tell the Earth spins by their pendulum swings."

Now 'Larry the liar' was turning all red
He took some deep breaths, and then calmly he said,
"What nonsense is this, should the moon wane or wax?
I say Brandywine is quite loose with the facts!

Will you fall for these negative nasty attacks,
From a man who HATES me and his friend brainiacs?
The truths that I tell you are chiseled in granite.
Elect Brandywine and he'll ruin the planet!"

A very thin child weighing only 3 stone
Struggled on to the stage, grabbed a loose microphone
And said; "I'll believe Mr. Larry for now
If he'll only tell us the manner of how

Mr Barleywine managed to so cleverly
First defy laws of motion, and then gravity."
And then something wonderful happened that day
For 'Larry the liar' had no more to say.

The rain promptly stopped and the sun began shining,
The clouds that were left had a bright silver lining.
Dip Barleywine won, you'll be happy to hear
And the people were prosperous many a year.

Allan Emery

Close Your Flowers

It dripped
cold today,

seeping quickly
slowly not quite liquid fast,

shivering from
bone to skin,

goose bumps quivering
arms and legs,

flaccid eyelids
now clung tight against

wicked blasts,
daffodils pressed down,

in the
cruel absence
of summer's roar;

an unexpected
static scorch.

Cp Culliton

JW.

The smoky room sank
into my clothes, staining
my grey top with the stink

of the busy casino atmosphere.
Chatter from the crowd
faded in and out as I pushed
my way through the throngs
of patrons waiting for the
chance to try their luck on

multicolored machines
making random noises. I
stepped into the quiet area,
empty food trays scattered
on salt and pepper tables,

kids screaming for drunk
parents. I lifted my eyes
to the bright pink neon sign -
Baskin Robbins. They settled

on you - milky brown skin, a
wide smile, glasses. My heart
nose dived as my eyes searched
your face again and again. A
cliché I once believed
impossible had come true.

I loved you.

Melissa Ingram

Number Ten

Ottmar plays;

number ten
of course.

Evening lights
hang over the canyon walls.

The cool sun shines the last of day's rays
through the softness of pine boughs

and you

you are on my mind
gliding with ease

across the kitchen floor
across the meadows of San Francisco

filling my heart till it overflows

in laughing tears of rememberance
fueling the promise of my return

holding you
for whom the promise is fulfilled.

In sweet dancing arms
I listen

the rhythm of life plays
across the canyon walls

chasing grace
step by sweet step.

Jamesvm

I Sit Through Her

April, 15th

I sit on the sofa
with a stare that could penetrate
an elephant, easily

holding my head from falling
with my hands, that I
imagine asking why

"I want you out by tomorrow"
or was there "would"
I try "what if" with several reasonable lines
until my mind and sight blurs again with numb disbelief

month ago everything was fine or
at least two...or four ago

"let's figure this out"
but how, I cannot figure

"I don't want to leave"
is the only reasonable line of
blur, I cannot

she must have said "or"
but what was the "or" for
could I just not go to it and
stay

she has been bit moody
"tomorrow" has to be
better, I can be, we can

April, 17th
I sit on the balcony
there was only one tomorrow

the one she showed me the dark
outside her door
row of them veiled in black

smoke of cigarette
emptiness is blazing flames that scorch the black
hell burns in me and in her little ears and eyes of resemblance
that leave me yelling at them without reason
that shin of hers on my child's face

I hate my children for awhile but it wont last

I want to hate them to hurt her

May, 5th
I can't sit
thoughts linger and weave them sticky webs on anything
"what about the kids?"

"I will take them from you" is a short cut of an idea leading to a
dead end faster than I can blink my eyes

bad choice of words
I'll quit, right now, this is the last cigarette

therapy?
would you just think about the kids?

is that all I got?

I'm trying to turn around a mind
that has moved on

just for the summer, for kids....

June, 23th

I sit on the bed

might as well lay

I will never find the strength to rise

I feel the void
and the pressure, pressure of void?

I texted to her that I'm not taking the kids this week, I'm busy
I smell the rotten cheese on the table
I remember a documentary
about survival in nature telling man can get by up to a month
without eating
I'll be okey
I have time
I find it hard to smell her anymore
I
no we

November, 15th
I sit on my knees
garage floor is cold and
there must be a tiny rock beneath my left knee

skies are clear
I am pouring,
the mobile fell into the ground
after the words
ringing, clinging, swinging, pointlessly shoving and grasping on
every nerve of my brain
"she's getting married"

I am a scene from a movie
knelt, exposed, indifferent and
they just keep pouring, nose too
I suddenly realize it has been seven months
and I haven't cried once
before

I enjoy the pouring and add
the weeping too

In the morning I wake up, cloudy outside
I smile

V.S. Paavolainen

How Poems Go

I really don't know how to tell
just how a poem turned out well,
or where the seeds of thought began.
There is no map, no master plan,
no brief instructions, laws or rules
for how to craft these little jewels.

I guess they start with where you live,
and who you see and what you give,
and somehow all that settles in—
somewhere inside,
where poems begin.

Some poems start inside the head,
and others in the heart instead,
but all those words converge and flow
through fingers—
that's how poems go.

And that is all I really know.

Katharine L. Sparrow

Shades Of Blue

On the shores of memories
Feeling various shades of blue
My feet and hands digging in the sand
Building a castle or two
One for me and one for you
Drowning my sorrows
Sinking in the moment
Wondering how and when
Years slipped through fingertips
Days washed away, dreams crushed
Dragged along like a prey
Folded, bent, moulded
Just another piece of clay
Silent tears evaporated in time
My life a portrait in silhouette

Essama Chiba

Summerhill

My gratitude is a green hill
Warm, soft, sunlit.
The wind speaks into grass
Calling out by name
And many names,
God, grace, Mama, family

And blue and blue and more blue
As wind lifts gaze
And changes hue.
Gratitude, compared with a summer day...

Deb Blondell-Pitt

Mine Alone

Somber? Peaceful ?
Tranquil. Respectfully done.
Closure here? Sure, closure.

Proper military ceremonies sedately accomplished,
attendants properly dressed,
remarks appropriate.

Memorial established,
complete with grand eulogy,
chest heaving sob and halting stepped exit –

Silent now --

Grass neatly trimmed.
Trees in park like casual placement,
Head stones ranked and filed

presided over by Eagle perched on marker –

markers in parade ground formation,
uniform, evenly spaced,
marching away over cloud kissed gentle slope,

to proceed unseen in endless numbers flowing in mind's eye
into the shrouding mist of memory.

"Our cause was just." ". . . sacrifice heroic."
"Selfless service that we all might . . ."

Oh, look. Not far off in neighboring fellowship, an older plot,
inscriptions dimmed by Nature's timeless hand;

and others elsewhere in careless scatter across the land
from conflicts fresh and unremembered--

sibling sanctuaries for remains of good intentions.

"In this place here, but not again!" ". . .not in vain."

"Oh, God!! Can this be a symbol of anguish?
How often a veiled, een wailing, mother, sister, wife -
stiff backed dad -- head bowed brother --
confused and melancholy child --

heavy stepped and hearted departed that day --
randomly returning, mist eyed,
empty tremble unshared, alone together, fresh blossom gently
placed?

How many forgotten causes, unborn children,
unattended weddings and proms, inventions never surfaced,
poems unwritten--generation after generation after generation ? ? ?

It matters not.

This is the unresolved final ending,
not for the entire world to know and see,
not for glory or guide-on raised,
not a collective symbol of community closure.

This is the unnecessary final note
in the unfinished symphony that was my child
-- my son -- my lovely girl.

Jack Mullen

Pokémon game of chance, play to save

In every tournament on ripple ground,
winners win losers loose the bound.

So in Pokémon game,
losers on the ladder of shame.

Some playing this game anywhere to wreck,
but this game so safe at home on line of neck.

The tickles chain so maim and dread,
on preys living lingering memories to be read.

Pokémon a game of chance,
players of fun and pun on battle frontier enhance.

A battle, a rattle by thyme,
warp heals all wounds at rhymes.

Now, the den of death,
flying pole to pillars in castle air beneath.

Cell phones a killer tool,
youngsters prime to ply on fun at fool.

We're as blinds walking corpse,
toying in the hands of death dive without a pulse.

The troy as an object and victim of error,
shouldn't walk in slippery and sinking sands of others but to look at
shades of mirror.

Ogbest Ezekiel

A Bearly Told Tale

A little girl with golden locks went, one day, for a walk,
was feeling rather lonely, and was looking just to talk.
She found a house deserted, and she peeked inside the door,
and in the kitchen found three chairs but there weren't any more.

She tried to climb upon the first, but it was far too tall,
the second one was not so good, and so she tried the small.
It felt so very comfortable she sat there for a while,
and at the corners of her mouth there played a little smile.

Now, sitting on the table were three bowls that had been filled,
she dipped into the biggest one; so hot! Some porridge spilled!
With caution dipped her spoon into the next bowl in the line,
but when she tried the third she found, it suited her just fine.

A yawn escaped and Goldilocks decided to count sheep,
the big bed was no good for her, its blankest in a heap,
the next bed had two pillows, and their angle was too steep,
a third she found to be just right, climbed on, and fell asleep.

Three bears came home, and Papa saw the mess someone had left,
then Mama saw the empty bowl, and Junior shouted 'theft!'!
Across the room so lightly came, the sound of gentle snore;
on Junior's bed, a little girl that no bear could ignore.

When Goldilocks awoke in fright, she tried to get away,
but Junior had a different thought, he wanted her to play,
when Goldilocks decided she would stay forevermore
the parent Bears renamed her, she became Bear Number Four!

Alf Collier

Sticky fingers

She knew how every color tasted
and blue was her favorite flavor frost
at Jackie's Corner where sign was pasted
to advertise sweet sherbets at low cost.

Italian ice filled in paper pockets,
with lemon, lime, or blueberry juice drink
that splashed with a spritzer like a rocket
about to leave in orbit from earth's brink.

Impressions of fruit crushes stay, linger,
in my mind in the summer when it's hot.
He licked the sugar off his sticky fingers,
I dropped a nickel in his tipping pot.

Laurie F. Grommett

Indian Summer

Long days of summer
come to pass
skies of water-colored glass
fades amethyst
to pearly white
Indian Summer,
gives way to night

Maria Oday

Keeping The Dream Alive

The sun shone through
an icy blaze, barely warming
the granite monuments surrounding
my father's final place of rest.

The Clinton Cemetery,
with waiting list,
people dying to get in,
anxious to mix floatsum
and jetsam with civil war
generals and university
presidents.

Since I knew I would never see
my father again,
from his grave I pilfered
two hardened clods,
sneaked them out in the pocket
of my woolen winter coat
then sobbed.

The walk back to the car felt
as if we were stumbling through
windblown evergreens chilled
by November's blatant frost.

The treachery of having
little material to show
for a life well lived, caused me
to experience a sort of highway
hypnosis as I shook the earth from
the hems of the pants belonging
to my only good suit.

James C. Allen

Finally

The wind wraps my chords
with a type of strangulation
which prevents a discernable
utterance.

Its chill has me stilled,
once the boy, the adult;
the aged privileged to speak
something close to the truth.

Do not assume good
has not been found,
this son I never had
never knew the longing
that my friends possessed.

He's not the prodigal,
look at who has come home,
to be bound into fatherhood
this fortunate time.

I tell him things he already knows,
he reminds,
he did not remain
an empty vessel those years
that saw me on my search.

And now dear boy,
while I still have the voice to sign
let me perform contortions,
my fingers twisted in ways uncountable.

They flash the same words,
despite the fog of life's confusing
war, the clearing smoke
wafts a gentle truth.

Love remains in quantities required
to fill us both.

James C. Allen

Dedicated to: Dean a close friend from Romania

Being single

Being single and ready to mingle,
I said to myself it is so easy;
but with the world full of strangers
and men whom you do not know
makes it very difficult.

Men out there with fake identities,
fake sob stories,
faking their way to trap you;
they con you with their sweet talks
and once you are ready
you learn you are being duped.

Tough being single,
and to find a man of your choice;
so with faith in Lord;
I leave it up to him
to find me a man or a soul-mate
one that will stand beside me
till the end.

Debra Joseph

Conception

the seven revolutions
a hopeful sperm
gifts his shimmery Earth's crust of an egg
immediately before conception

as immaculate as
sunlight

Deb Blondell-Pitt

[Waltz] Ae Freslighe

Sonnet verse casts silhouettes
immortal dancing devil.
Amber braids wreathe pirouettes
love's muse, salutes mirths revel.

Kiss, soft touch, a serenade
arouses bliss filled chorus.
Maidens blush past promenade
desiring dance in forest.

Moon of azure, wandering
consumes delight upon it.
Marriage of mind's pondering
sweet memories of sonnet.

Chrysanthy Pappas

A Woman

There was,
in the dark,
a woman,
who did not know love,
who did not know my love.

There was,
in the dark,
a valley,
that did not flourish,
nothing blossomed,
nothing bloomed.

There was,
in the light,
a gleaming fire,
which consumed this savage animal,
which sparked this vacant hole.

There was,
in the dark,
a woman,

who
s   h
a   t   r
t   e   e
r   d

what once was whole.

Abigail van Eden

Forever Young

Hold my hand
To the end of time
Travel with me
To a faraway land
Where sand
Is made of gold
Rivers filled
With honey and milk
There I'll wear
A green satin robe
Crown my hair
With silver flowers
Put on a necklace
Of pearls in rows
Drink in a crystal glass
From endless streams
Of eternal peace
In everlasting love
Forever young

Essama Chiba

"Just friends"

My heart is comprised
Of the history
of our impossible love
I wrote you many notes
with my sincere words
Never believing that your heart
would not reciprocate
My sweet notes
Oh !
someone help me ,my lord !
Listen to my voice
To my prayers
My heart became fragile
like an old piece of paper
every letter which held a picture of you
I hid that book in my heart
Like a precious jewel
I've built walls around it
Made with crystals and rocks
I've traveled
across seas for you
My lost lover
But what you did you give in return ?
We're not the same
My love
Because you did nothing
Except tear my letters
By saying we should be "just friends "

Maissa Laadhar

Harvest Time

As the farmer gathers in the hay,
piling golden bales roof-high in the barn,
and stores potatoes and apples
in the cool, dry cellar,
thankful to God and the weather,
so it is with me, my daughter,
as you say good-bye to us,
looking back with a wave
and a tentative smile
as you enter a new door,
to be greeted by unfamiliar faces.

It was hard work, yes,
these seventeen years,
the daily-paid mortgage of love.
But as with the farmer
who has labored over many a crop that failed
from too much rain or not enough,
or gophers or rabbits or deer or birds
or insects or hail or tornadoes or fire,
or timing just plain gone wrong,
who sees this year, this crop
is safe in the barn,
so it is with me, my daughter,
as you leave me to learn
other lessons from other teachers.
You are young and beautiful and perfect;
we have made it, you and we,
the entire village of folk who have cared for you
from birth to now, by the grace of God,
and we celebrate and rejoice
and grieve a little for the passing
of a perfect season.

Susanne Donoghue

Seeds of Love

The clouds enveloped me
Your love is deep to the core

Spinning like a whirlybird
Carrying seeds through the distance
On the wind enclosed in pairs

Dropping a little each moment
Finding its way to the river

Growing ever green
A Mediterranean maple tree

My spirit a force of nature
Full of strength and endurance

Bathing freely in sunrays
Enlightenment purifies my soul

Essama Chiba

Her Garden Grows

In the garden
Grows knowledge
and wisdom, beauty and grace-
In the fullness of its harmonious melodies
And in living color
There is goodness, freedom and healing in her peace
In the garden-

Andrea Owens

On the airport

The plane landed,
it is 3am, the airport is pretty empty,
I collected my baggage and step out,
There are few people that have come to meet their
loved ones or friends,
me I am standing alone,
wondering how to get home.

From a distance I see an airport representative,
he is coming towards me,
He asked me mam do you want a hotel,
I said no I need a cab,
he asked to me to wait.

He returned with a cab,
he put my bags in, and
seated himself with the driver
and we began the drive home.

We did not talk for a while,
he asked me from where I had come,
then we were silent.

We drove for an hour and finally reached,
he helped me with my bags
he then said bye and left,
then it struck me - why he drove along with me.

He turned to look at me once more before going,
I smiled at him and went in.
I did not stop thinking of him,
there is something I felt for him.
But that night in the wee hours was
the first time I met my love
and finally married him after six and half years.

Debra Joseph

The Dawning Of Despair

The tall grass screams cut to her roots
by the jagged teeth slung with savage force.

Sun sparkles from the polished blade,
illuminating pride, pleased with the efficiency
of the deed.

The cuttings line the field,
lifeless soldiers at the conclusion
of battle.

Let's not make too much of it,
people will think the metaphor
refers to something understandable.

Death is easy, the process hard.
Two years today I watched
him work, clean as a whistle
simple as mowing the yard.

The corpse of love lay warm
in the bed,
the horror in my guts
rising to a shattering note.

Something broke in my heart,
fragile as crystal
something I knew that even time
could not repair.

James C. Allen

Poet Laureate

with might and main

i enter
like an olympic medalist

into the dingy dark room
reserved only

for the greatest.

all eyes reverse
in my direction
as i pull out
the old yellow script

once again
savoring every word.

i continue
feeling their hunger
and for a few brief moments

i take center stage

the swirling smoke
and the stench
of their drunken breath

is all that respires...

...one seems to hesitate

dangling like a halo
around my head

caressing my hair

like an old whore
reminiscing lost youth

forcefully she tries
to writhe back
into her papery
pleated skin.

a wry smile
curls upon my lips

knowing

this will be
my only chance

to fuck her!

Chrysanthy Pappas

The Reminder

Obscuring Mist will seasonally descend
with its grayness and chilling moisture,
distinguishing not time and place,
for joy or sadness.

The Eagle,
strong, symbolic, independent,
chooses what and where alone
for survival, security of nest--
perhaps for a moment to regroup or rest from
hunt or exploration.

Good Earth,
set aside for final rest by people,
In respect and memory within tribe and family,
knows nothing of how and why it accrues a special value
in hearts and minds.

But we stand witness to a slice of time and place, and creature
when no creative hand combined these elements in nature,

by chance here captured by camera in hand or of the mind,
that seems to harmonize a perfection of purpose,
a statement of universal meaning,
a mood of pause in crisis,
in scope both personal and communal.

No ordinary field, this place,
to carry the generational tale of the ordinary, the regular, the
general.
Rather, a plot,
carefully selected to commemorate particularly the extra-ordinary,
who passed away in unchosen place or circumstance,
to pay the price,
that those remaining may think, breathe and live free.

A Veteran's cemetery here,

Damp, grey stones bearing weather worn words of whom and
when,

grassed and graveled,
iron fenced and gated,
annually flagged and flowered.

And this instant,

visited by lone Eagle, The American Eagle,
perched upon mist shrouded, dampened, cold as the grave,
stone marker,

this moment, stands as a Reminder.

In neutral nature's setting,
Past and Present,
Symbol and Reality,
exist in our hearts and minds
as either challenge or hopeless gesture of defeat.

With end of race fatigue, sweat soaked in exhaustion,
drained and pain strained,
runner and soldier, mothers, wives and sisters,
orphaned children and still living battle crippled and maimed,
those unscarred and some untried,
may choose:

Shall I rise and strive or fall and fail?
Shall I carry on or surrender, proceed or quail?

Thanks to this moment,
the instant

--the tabloid Reminder, from mist and stone and bird combined—

those who will press on with torch held high,
passed "with failing hands,"

are strengthened beyond the call to melt in the mist—

will find in the Reminder

that weariness is a tiny price
against payments already made.

And when all else is gone but the strength of spirit and will
to keep alive the promise to mankind
of freedom and dignity, birth right freely given,

Torch bearers will know, all will be preserved
only with duty done and honor sustained,

Reminded of

their noble quest,
their debt,
their mission,

the Blessing of their lives.

Jack Mullen

Eighteen

Slip out of a moonless night
and into lacy underwear.
Bite my lip,
take a sip
of this poppy-tonic and
wipe the cartoons from the screen.

Clear history.

Thuds of books, thumbing
through sums and scrawly notes.
The sprawl of stars are
inside my backpack.
Skip church. I'm pondering
our condition and what life means.

Mountain's shadowy light.
Think back to the cigarette that night
and how this time-tinder
burns bendy youth to cinder.
I stumped it out. Serves me right.
A sooty kind of clean.

Destined to dull
into mediocre routine.
I will ash away –
from this eighteen.

Beth Keryn

Life Death and Love

What does it mean to live?
To die?
To love?
To listen to the wind dancing with the leaves
as the sun rises and falls?
Seek not beauty and seek not to be beautiful
and there you shall be overcome by the effortless beauty;
that just is
and is forever.
Let your heart weep
like the crying of the snow
when winter withers.
The beauty in love transcends both life and death;
thus I shall love you as I live
and I shall love you as I die
and I want for nothing more.

Mark Moir

Wilderness Star

Great wilderness in quiet lies-
Peacefully, my minds chatter stills.
Steady the heart of Mother Earth-
Sacred her mountain joy I cross;
Thunderous pace of silence peak,
Cadence of primal shift in time.
Swells my wonder renewed bright shines.
Her star is the star in my eye.

Andrea Owens

Our own elsewhere

Anchored fast
to a swaying cube of slowly molten
steel and glass

We stood erect
on a shimmering silver firing line

The thin, obese, fathers, mothers,
brothers, sisters.
Recorded, in a single instant,

indelible now
a scar on world consciousness

Shivering, we bowed before the falsest dawn.
our city rising through dust & fire.

Heads erect, arms outstretched
unwilling martyrs
hanging on a twisted flaming crucifix

Then it came
the flailing tide of reaping storms.

Jump.
Fly.
in burning skies.

and die below
in our own elsewhere.

Dave Kavanagh

Because I am the only one!

I can never be no-one, because I am the only one!
Who is that unique me that's replaceable by none!

You say you could easily replicate me as my clone,
But it would not be a real me, only one mere drone.

I live in singularity, yet the infinite-self lies within me,
I'm part of the timeless world; past, present, yet to be.

I am bonded into relationships with my kith and kin,
That wouldn't be just the same even if I had a twin.

I think and feel like no other does, you like it or not,
I have left my mark on the world, a soft sweet spot.

If I weren't there, a difference it would surely make,
What I have said and done, no one could ever fake.

When I am no more there, I might be soon forgotten,
I'd be woven in the thread of time, as a wisp of cotton.

The seeking eyes would always find me in my imprints,
Connect and my eternal presence will give you my hints.

I was there when we were created; I will be there forever,
Times and places would change, my identity would never.

We, the seeds of eternity, in God's eyes were perfectly sown,
Our bodies are of glass to be broken, our soul is forever own.

So let us treasure each other as one of a kind, just as we are,
We all shine in the galaxy of creation, each one of us is a star.

Why should then we think of becoming adversaries not friends,
When we're paintings of the same colors in our distinct blends.

Let us live in eternal peace, whoever and wherever we may be,
Because we know we are the only ones, whether it's you or me!

Dr. Asghar Nazeer

Thoughts of Fall

A curl of wood smoke, apple-spiced,
twists toward the stars, emerging—
a looming moon, like candle's glow
with chilly night converging.
The insects trill a timid song,
as if they can't remember
the lyrics of a summer's night,
chased off by late September.
And as the earth's face turns around
to warm the southern oceans
my melancholy musings turn
to circumspect devotions.
A yielding sigh, my breath plumes out
beneath the starry sprawl—
I turn and head back to the house,
my thoughts tucked in to fall.

Katharine L. Sparrow

Rain

It rained last night,
the mausoleum of stars was silent,
no sound except dripping,
and the echoes were strident

the green grew upon the dark,
even the tree's swelled with water,
as the moon grew gibbous
and wetly watched
as the rain fell in rivulets
flooding curved roads

everything was sodden,
the earth swam with clogged leaves,
spiraling toward choked drains

movement flowed,
in sinuous coils, snakelike,
and undulating through damp grass,
still the water slid, heeding none,
seeking its own path,

no sound except dripping,
and the odor rose damply,
of rich earth and trees,

it rained last night,
clouds grey still shed their burden,
and when morning comes,
damp and sodden,
Plath's sheep huddle disconsolately together,
waiting,

no sound except the steady dripping,
and the woods are green again.

Corvus-corax

The Flag [sonnet XXXVI]

Above the swirl of death, I swore I felt
A chill foreboding carried on the wind,
As reeling from a blow that he was dealt,
The standard bearer fell beneath the din.
His banner, more than words, upheld our soul,
Its trampled colors bleeding into clay;
A symbol of defiance conquest stole,
Forgotten where the dying soldier lay.
Along the fringe where cravens crept, I crept
And anguished over what was almost won.
I watched, unseen, the massacre and wept;
My honor perished with those on the lawn.
I left, and lived and loved and wed and died
A wretch the flag I kept could never hide.

William Kenneth Keller

Seasons

The seasons' change from summer heat to fall
my grandpa saw one-hundred times in all!
At first it's very subtle; breezes chilled
which bring a dampened smell of earth that's tilled.
The ants invading homes for months on end,
all suddenly they disappear -- descend
retreating to their subterrane dirt homes;
they leave to live in rooted worlds of gnomes.
Then, almost to the day of fall's equinox,
the nights get cold, they enter -- keen, cunning fox!
More blankets needed, coats for early morn,
our sun he rises later, all forlorn.
Strong winds appear; abrupt, abundantly,
as if to say, "I'm here, get used to me!"

Karen Lee Gilbert Eisenlord

Keeping The Dream Alive

The sun shone through
an icy blaze, barely warming
the granite monuments surrounding
my father's final place of rest.

The Clinton Cemetery,
with waiting list,
people dying to get in,
anxious to mix floatsum
and jetsam with civil war
generals and university
presidents.

Since I knew I would never see
my father again,
from his grave I pilfered
two hardened clods,
sneaked them out in the pocket
of my woolen winter coat
then sobbed.

The walk back to the car felt
as if we were stumbling through
windblown evergreens chilled
by November's blatant frost.

The treachery of having
little material to show
for a life well lived, caused me
to experience a sort of highway
hypnosis as I shook the earth from
the hems of the pants belonging
to my only good suit.

James C. Allen

Lavender blooms

Lavender blooms, come grace again,
of beauty in ethereal,
whispers swaying in the breeze,
my broken heart to heal,
no sunset on a harvest sky,
soothe my heart's dull ache,
a longing for my love's return,
this lilac bloom doth take,
it's scent upon the wing of prayer,
to my lover's heart,
awaken passion once again,
this bloom my love impart

Gassingon

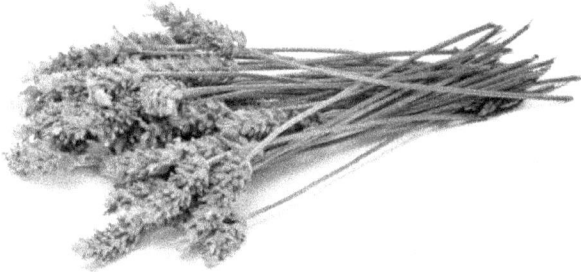

Ode to Art

Art is the universe in motion reflected in the human hearts longings- it's creative mirror is music that touches the source of soul-enlightens inspires and empowers the human spirit to greatness-it's passions move humanity ever forward.

Andrea Owens

forte

pigment's
palette
etched a passage
painted white
with hues
of vesper's song

softly roping braille

and writing
stamps unseen
upon the latitude of my cross

a journey breathed
astride old grey

destined for returns
echoed back to you

until then

i rest

within the forte
of solitude

while silence reigns
as comforter

a courteous old friend

until then
the eminence
of peace resounds

Chrysanthy Pappas

November Noise

For my late brother, Daniel Ingram
August 24, 1993 - November 23, 2015

I yelled at you today.
No, you weren't around to hear it.
But it didn't matter.

I was fast asleep in my warm bed, and you came to me in a dream.
Your head was no longer smashed. You were standing too, glowing
like the sun. You smiled and laughed, because you didn't know. I
don't remember what happened next. Dreams are like that - random,
fleeting. A lot like my emotions as a teenager, dating boys who
simply wanted to use me. Oh, how you hated them. You were
younger than me, but that didn't mean you didn't feel responsible
for my heart's well-being. Like the time I screamed into a humid
August night laced with gnats, upset with one of these boys. He was
no man, in fact, you were more of a man than him, seven years his
junior, and you called mom to come over, save my soul, scared for
my sanity. That's something mom lost the day we saw you; cold,
unmoving, no longer among the living. She hasn't been the same
since you left us behind. I say you got lucky, went up to meet the
Lord before us. Of course, sometimes that feels like a lie. It wasn't
luck, at least not the good kind. Why were you driving 60 in a 25? I
need to know.

I yelled at you today.
You're no longer around to hear it.
But I'll just go ahead and believe you did anyway.

Melissa Ingram

Patriotic Streamers

& Pyrotechnic Dreams

Patriotic streamers
covered the parade.
Which ended at park center
under cool Maples shade.

Chicken and ribs
sweetly scented the air
around sticky faced children
with cotton candy hair.

A barber shop quartet
completed the scene.
Lulling senior citizens
into a nostalgic dream.

Their four part harmony
danced through the air.
With red striped straw hats
lending, an authentic flair.

Blankets and lawn chairs
covered the park,
as the festivities paused
with the coming of dark.

Orchestra in place
kettle drums at the ready.
For a pyrotechnic dream
thunderous and heady.

Silver sand sparkled
as it fell from the sky
while onlookers smiled
with a twinkling eye.

Children all shouted
cheering at the sight
of this magical sky
on a midsummer night.

Parents caught in a memory
from a time long ago
when they first saw fireworks
with their faces aglow.

Vicarious reliving
through euphoric recall
they were once again children
in awe of it all.

With a thunderous grand finally
and the cannons loud clap
all the babies were wailing
in full diapers of crap.

That was my queue
to the car now we go
to beat the mad rush
at the end of the show.

With a smile and a sigh
we rushed past all the cars
in the land of the free
under blanket of stars.

William J. Reed IV

the narrowest rings~

there is a tree-
grieving leaves,

calligraphed in
vibrant colors,

a life-story
carried in veins

I collect them
faster than they fall

so not to forget
summer,   and,
neglect to remember
fingers birthing flowers

before scarred

there is a tree-
grieving leaves,

calligraphed in
vibrant colors,

a life-story
carried in veins

I collect them
faster than they fall

so not to forget
summer,   and,
neglect to remember
fingers birthing flowers

before scarred

crumbs.of.sorts.

Until Tomorrow

This forest of family trees
keeps her tethered
to the shadows
as she waits
to hear him dream

bound to the night
only to be the light
to his moon
and place the stars
beneath his pillow

so in the morning
he shall awake
with the beauty of her tune
and be granted the strength
to create his own dawn.

Delilah White

Beside the Crimson Moon (Quatern)

She brushed beside the crimson moon
and blew a balm of breathy kiss.
It's then you heard her honeyed tune,
a fairy's song of soothing bliss.

Each night new birds flew near her wings
that brushed beside the crimson moon,
they fluttered as lost kites on strings
and hovered as the spring in June.

Her silhouette, a fly cocoon,
shaped shadow 'gainst the midnight sky.
It brushed beside the crimson moon
embodying a lullaby.

The meadow bathed in music's light.
Her voice was blessed with silver spoon.
The notes she sparked brought sheer delight
when brushed beside the crimson moon.

Laurie F. Grommett

The Loving Butterfly

Sitting by the window
I was looking outside
to see nothing
with the mind
restless, sad.
Monotony was
swallowing me,
annoyance irritating!
I was struggling
with them with fail.
All on a sudden
a butterfly came
and sat on my hand.
The glossy wings
with colourful colours
and its innocent love
took me to the heaven of joy
driving sadness, monotony
away from me.

Sidhan Roy

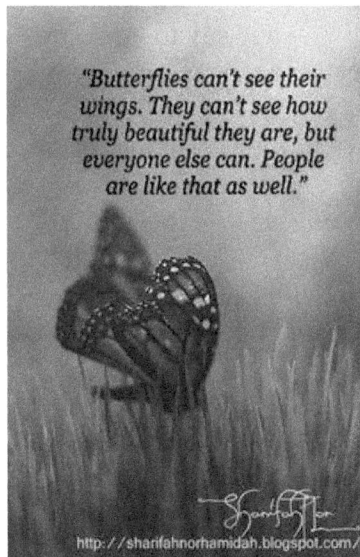

"Butterflies can't see their wings. They can't see how truly beautiful they are, but everyone else can. People are like that as well."

http://sharifahnorhamidah.blogspot.com/

What Love is ...

Love is the most powerful thing in life
Love is a sweet disease
unhealed addiction

love is when you see the whole universe
in the eyes of someone
love is when you are sitting alone
feeling the cold and the pain
and suddenly you feel the warmth
of a sweet kiss on your head

love is when you are afraid of something
and someone gives you a hand
to overcome your fears and make it ends
love is when you catch a cold
and you find someone to make for you
a hot soup

love is when you feeling lost
and your tears streaming down on your cheeks
you will find that someone
drying your tears
and say to you
everything will be alright my dear

love is when your hair is messy
with no makeup on
and wearing your pajamas to sleep

you will hear those sweet words
"you look like a beautiful queen "
And remember that
your first love is your mother
keep that in mind my darling

Maissa Laadhar

Bassiph and Calissavend

The elves roaming the forest floor are difficult to see,
With flesh in shades of verdant green they hide in any tree,
With spears sharpened to needlepoint they hunt both night and day,
For beetle's luminescent shells and toads along the way.

Bassiph is stronger than the rest, so leads the merry band
Of elves and sometimes pixie folk across this magic land.
Where maidens fair and beautiful weep for their prince to save,
And rescue them from gothic towers or yet, an early grave.

The wizards on the mountainside and witches in the dells,
Keep Bassiph busy all the day collecting for their spells
And spying in the King's royal court Bassiph must be alert,
Of friends that are among the knights and foes he should divert.

Skulduggery is at its worst when knights seek damsels fair,
So young Bassiph is sent for charms and magic spells where'er.
That's when the wizard conjures up enchantments to enflame -
And if by dawn the spells don't work Bassiph gets all the blame!

Bassiph is not alone in this he has Calissavend,
A sprite he rescued long ago when close to his life's end,
No bigger than a grasshopper, no smaller than a fly
He sits atop Bassiph's tall hat watching the world go by.

He sees such things Bassiph can't see of dangers way ahead,
Beyond and o'er the mountainside where green elves fear to tread,
For yonder from the western sky there lies the mortal's land,
Where deeds performed by wizardry are hard to understand.

Lulu Gee

travelers

ragged clothes,
weary eyes,
this day fades
in your dusty beard

you've walked
around those mountains
where Shiva still lingers
and mazes of the wind
find their way to past
you've touched the essence
of those overbloomed meadows
where evening breeze
caresses your virgin desires
but
your smile
hides the gravity
of those men in saffron
whose eyes betray the truth
that
not all sins dissolve
in the waters of ganga

so
while sitting beside the highway,
waiting for a god in exile
who will agree to accompany you
to a brand new beginning,
you contemplate
the color of destruction
gray
and smile over the realisation
that philosophy doesn't evade you anymore
and that
blue is how we measure sadness

sipping tea

in an ugly corner
that won't hold its breath for you,
you finally understand life;
a father
lends his bruised heart
to his only son
and scars travel through time
like unanswered questions

so you hide your stories
at the corner of your lips,
smile at strangers with broken empathy,
sing a song
sing a song
and walk back home
with renewed understanding
that
dying on the roads
doesn't make you a traveler

Alpha Centuari AKA Aishwarya

To Where and Why?

Why do I always feel this way?
My world in total disarray,
dull care you leave me so alone
on this my lost, dejected throne.
Where now I ask, to where and why?
Where nothing seems to satisfy.

Barry Hopkins

Karma's knitted knots...

You and I are crinkles in the page of time.
You and I are twinkles that blink in rhyme.

You and I live in the tiniest pores of history.
You and I give canniest clues to its mystery.

You and I perceive ages, in lifetime so brief.
You and I leave ashes, incinerated in grief.

You and I are horizon for sun to rise and set.
You and I are heaven, where stars first met.

You and I are the glow on the face of moon.
You and I are flow of space in sky's lagoon.

You and I reside in a ripple, dying on a river.
You and I hide in a bubble, sighing in quiver.

You and I are whispers of a blushing breeze.
You and I are glimmers of dew adoring trees.

You and I are nagging no, yearn yielding yes.
You and I are sagging snow, sculpting stress.

You and I are one yet alone in every moment.
You and I are none, but known in any instant.

You and I are links in loops of destiny's dots.
You and I are kinks of karma's knitted knots.

Dr. Asghar Nazeer

Zikr

The doors are open
To those who travel in love

My spirit a mirror
Reflecting Your Light

My body a drop of rain
A tear of devotion

I whisper Your name
With each beat of my heart

Chanting in a rhythmic repetition
Dissolving into music of the spheres

Vivid tones orbiting round the stars
In harmony with the cosmos

Your presence illuminate my soul
I vanish from myself become an atom

Between us there are no goodbyes
There are no us, there is only You

Essama Chiba

The Old & The Sea

He wished to swim, but the winter had approached faster than ever before. The scent of the sea breeze he once submerged himself into during his youth began smelling more and more like frigid air--how it burned his nostrils. No fluttering birds flew overhead, only phantoms of his boyhood that dissipate into fog once he averts his yearning gaze, struggling to repress every fun moment exuding warmth that his hands has lost long ago. He sighs lightly as the bronze shards of sand beneath his walking cane begin to shift softly with his parting footsteps. The horizon, in slow motion, begins to paint itself in wonderful reds, tinting his white hair a nostalgic sunset hue. As he staggers away from the waves becoming colder and colder while crisp autumn leaves fall one by one, he waves his hand to the currents that once cradled him kindly. The sun disappears into the other side of the world as his footsteps become washed away, like the remaining memories of the boy who pretended to breathe underwater during the fading summer.

althaia

The antique set

An old convent I visited
as I am invited to tea,
in the parlor I am seated;
and set my eyes on the table nearby,
the table were laden with antique
pot and pans and some lovely china ware.

A delight to see her possess these,
the nun saw me staring at the tea-set
and said it was a gift on her birthday
from her late mother.

Debra Joseph

Journey Within

Love steps on sandy beaches
washed away by waves
like childhood dreams;

yet dreams were woven in eyes
like an eye-liner
diluted with cries.

Summer months dry up life
Spring came and bade adieu
Winter weaves a fog-liner;

matured love hides no pangs
to eternity it flows
through the Milky Way.

morning, evening
I walk down the bay
in setting sun's glow,

searching lost footsteps,
a journey within
to you, Eternity.

Rajkumar Mukherjee

My Love is a Star

My love is a star
That envelopes everything
Within its firmament
In gentle warmth
And illumination.

A self-sustaining star,
To light my world
For all eternity,
In tenderness of heart.

My star brings purpose
And actual identity
To the tear-filled spaces
Of sorrowful joy.

My blessed guiding star
Calls forth pure grace
By her unique charms
As I mirror divine,
Enchanted empathy.

Allan Emery

The Seasons

Summer-
Blue ocean, orange sky,
green surf, hazel eyes. I walk
the beach, stick my pale toes in
the sand, dig deeper, trying to find
my soul. I lose myself, feel out of place.
These moments help me escape.

Fall-
We lost you in the fall,
random, unexpected. Your
blood ran red, or so I imagined.
The blood stained the concrete where
they placed your smashed car. It matched
your head. Now you're dead.

Winter-
Blurry through my tears, the
snow fell white on the dry brown
leaves. The road was slick, the blacktop
no longer visible. I crashed on my way to work.
I wasn't used to driving in these conditions. Maybe
you weren't either.

Spring-
New life blossoms, yet you
remain underground as the pink
and red bloom, and the grass grows greener.
We placed your headstone, months after the fact.
We still hoped it was a dream. Now the seasons begin
again.

Melissa Ingram

When lovers are lost into each other!

Love birds can spend the night in each other's arms,
lying by the shore,

Dreaming of making those moments eternal,
yet keep begging for more.

When lovers are lost into each other,
their hearts keep riding the waves,

And create ripples that scribble their love story in water;
until it engraves.

Who can read love stories etched in the drifting pages
of flowing water?

To do that you need a tender heart that feels,
not a mind that is smarter.

Love lights up our lives,
just like the sun spreads sunshine in the day,

Though Apollo dazzles with a light burst,
Venus' charm is just one ray.

Lovers die but love lives forever,
as it is the sacred knot that binds souls,

The fable of love remains the same;
yet another couple replays its roles.

When you're in love,
world gets bigger but there's only one other than you,

While you two are together, whoever else is around,
you don't have a clue.

Not everyone in this universe gets so lucky
to meet a loving life partner,

And then like they say in the fairy tales,
be able to live happily ever after.

Many a hapless souls fall in love
with someone who returns no affection,

And end up with broken hearts;
as they're too delicate to endure rejection.

If you are amongst the lucky few
who have yet found your true soul-mate,

Then no matter how difficult are the times,
hold on to that gift of your fate.

Your love is the magic that will be enough
to tide over life's ups and downs,

Whether destiny forces you to live clad in rags
or bestows you with crowns.

Just like at the beginning of times there was the land,
and there was sea,

Since then they've been always next to each other;
and forever they'll be!

Dr. Asghar Nazeer

Sweet Rebellion

She is celestial -
the mother of the galaxy
with an expanding girth,
subtly dipping out of orbit
in a lunar revolution,
spilling bright epiphanies
in profound slivers of scintillation,
each beam an offspring
streaming from her soft brilliance
across the fringes of night,
molten by a deviating sun.

Her halo befits her like a crown,
the aura of her
lucent silhouette inspiring
constellations – as they borrow
a portion of her quintessential
light, the opalescence
perfectly mirrored in the
lux of each singular star.

Like mercury she quivers,
as her shimmering silver drops
disperse, painting twilight
with stardust confetti,
then having lulled the
universe to sleep,
she dreamily ascends,
settling into her
blanket of sky.

skkingrey

Butterfly

Maybe I've been through more
maybe I've been through less
maybe I've seen it all...
at my very best.
Over thought
under thunk
been high & sober...
been low & drunk.

Did I fail?
Did I pass the test?
Who wrote the questions?
Did I answer it at best?
All we are is lookin' for a reason
tryin' to make sense of what we believe in
always second guessing
if even for a moment...
like a butterfly we flutter
and when we all die
it doesn't matter...

to anyone but the dirt
the ocean the sky
to anyone but the builder...
so what is it from which you hide?...

the dirt that makes you
the dirt that takes you
then makes you again.
Don't ever be afraid to live your life.
Don't ever be afraid to die.
Be afraid not to live,
while you're alive
Butterfly.

Alison Emery

Compadres

Driving east last night
I shared the moon's delight
as she rose straight up from the horizon
to light my way home.
Newly aware of owls
and the patience of trees,
I considered the glory
of the company I keep
in this amazing dance of stars and planets
we're caught up in.

Neighbors and friends
fascinating creatures
of every stripe and stink,
mountains and trees,
canyons, winds, and seas,
all the children and their parents,
we whirl together round the sun.
By myself, I am unnoticeable,
but then,
I have never been alone.

Susanne Donoghue

Sci fi love

Relaxed sorrowness,
Electromagnetic contact
Transferred happiness

Rnayak

Bardo

To the point of no return
To the hollow dark passage
Where we all fear to tread
Bardo, the land of the unknown
Death is a great master
Could teach us how to live
We drown into the moment
As if there is no tomorrow
We abandon yesterday
We ask too man questions
Raising only doubts
Uncertain, do we or don't we
Have the freedom of choice
We didn't choose to be born
We don't choose to die
Yet all what's in between
Is up to us to define
Which path to take
How to understand
That life is a gift♡

Essama Chiba

Superman

I saw Superman in the sky
who said ' I am learning to fly '
He hit a big rock,
which was quite a shock.
A good job that he cannot die.

Barry Hopkins

Prisoners in their own minds...

Do you know anyone who has been handed down a life sentence?
Someone so innocent who can't commit a crime even in pretense?

The cruelty of this punishment is to be locked inside your own mind!
Unable to tell what happens in the isolation cell you've been confined!

You may have loving people around you to look after, as they care,
But left guessing what you need, as your desires you cannot share.

What you think no one knows, what others think you do not know,
Your only interpreter is a loving heart that recognizes your yes or no.

You want to say a lot, struggling to catch thoughts in turbulent flow,
They keep racing, changing tracks; sans brakes to make them slow.

You hear whatever is being said to you and see what's being shown,
But since you can't get your words across, so many leave you alone.

When you've fallen sick, what you're going through remains unknown,
For every pain and grief you suffer, the only language to tell is a groan.

Unique thoughts of a beautiful mind and pure feelings of a lovely heart,
You can't share with your own kind as if you and they are worlds apart.

By now you'd have surely guessed I am talking of the severely autistic,
Letting you imagine their malady, let me say why I am so pessimistic.

As time passes by, these prisoners in their own minds keep increasing,
No one knows what locks them up, and is there any way for releasing?

These inmates may have numerous visitors, who they can't really meet,
The more their well-wishers come closer to them, the more they retreat.

They've their stories to tell and heart-touching autobiographies to write,
But don't know how to speak their hearts and minds; isn't that a plight?

These angels belong to paradise, but held hostages in an unkind world,
We've to set them free while they live alone among us like a caged bird.

If more and more of our generations keep withdrawing into alienation,
We might start asking, is giving lifeless-life the purpose of procreation?

For centuries mankind evolved into better thinkers and communicators,
Why watch ruthlessly ravaging regression before finding why it occurs?

As the river of destiny flows through time, more children keep drowning,
We can't close our eyes saying it's their parents' problem, while frowning.

I beg you whoever and wherever you are to help in freeing these captives,
Politicians, researchers and philanthropists! Do change your perspectives.

Seeking your attention are poverty, hunger, disease, all kinds of suffering,
They're all important in their own right, so I must be reasonable in asking.

When you are allocating your time and money among ones who deserve,
Just a minute of your time and a cent of wealth, for autistics you reserve!

Dr. Asghar Nazeer

I'm relatively ugly.

Einstein had a theory about energy and mass,
But I've come back to tell you, he can stick it up his ass.
Relatively speaking when travelling through space,
Your insides become outsides and squiggle up your face,
You ears turn into jelly moulds and wobble up and down,
And when you try to smile real hard,
your grin becomes a frown,
Your hair drops out, your teeth go pink,
your brains seep through your ears,
So thanks to dear old Albert I've come back in arrears..

Barry Hopkins

metamorphosis

We all have baggage, burdens we must bear,
From all the tribulations of our past,
Fraught with anxiety because we care,
And palpable regret that's sure to last.
Responsibility for all we've done,
Full ownership for all our sordid ways,
As we've endeavored to reach number one
Preparing to succeed despite the haze.
Yet, we are living in this moment now,
And who we were has learned and thought and grown
Forgiveness is the vaunted process how
We see we are not now the selves we've known.
Take all the selves you were and cast them far
Tend only to the consciousness you are.

Allan Emery

A Metaphor for Diversity

A pinwheel
As a child, my favorite toy for Spring
Mom and I constructed it together
On that one day, she was all mine for real.

Cardboard and paint… yet it needed
Love, care, devotion, and careful hands
Spinning wildly on a breezy day
if it could have flown alone, its path led to the stars

I wonder about the allure of a pinwheel
It has other names…whirligig, buzzer, spinner
Shakespeare uses the Pinwheel as a warning--
What goes around, comes round…that's the deal

What a metaphor for man's diversity!
Twirling yet waiting for the next brush of wind
Glossy and dazzling or pastel and sedate
The duality of reminding man of the balancing of life forces

Chinese wisdom—pinwheel turns a man's luck
when he faces adversity

Carol Davis

Shadows on the Wind

I

Rays of dawn, on forest lawn, shadow woodland trees,
through distant hills, autumn fills,
bright orange tinted leaves...

II

As winter's snow, in whispers blow, waiting seasons end,
sad fairies sing, as geese take wing,
like shadows on the wind...

III

Where mice at play, this fall-like day, scurry to and fro,
in mirrored hues, neath skies clear blue,
as fragrant breezes blow...

IV

This deepn'd hush, in autumn's blush, with colors all ablaze,
fairies dream of summer's scene, in saddn'd yesterdays,
cool eve of night, in September's light wakes,
to faded grays...

V

Dying flowers, like passing hours, seem shadows on the wind,
like falling leaves, from ancient trees,
as prisms brightly blend...

VI

Cloudless skies, in twilight cries,
goodbye...to summer's end...

Melody Hamby Goss

Novel By The Shore

I lay her on soft down,
next to the edge of the iridescent sea,
diamondesque as sunlight
illuminating lacy froth at the foot
of her form.

A final kiss on her still pink lips,
a smattering regret combined
with relief,
there is no redemption in exaggerated
suffering.

Even though denied I knew every
crime committed,
names, places, dates;
the lost desires the misplaced
devotions.

In her graying hands,
the manuscript of her final write
ink running now as cool waves
began to lap the truth from those
pages of life's piercings.

The title written in pencil
would remain as testament
to the indelible wrongs.
it read like a thermometer
whose last degree had been reached,
the recipe of essential ingredients
washed from the conclusion
resting before us now,
it read:
"How To Kill A Poet"

James C. Allen

The Wind Of Change

As I sail soft currents
I'm blown by a change of winds
Attracted within magnetic fields
My being disintegrates
Torn between East and West

Shaken to the core
I attempt to recollect broken pieces
Of my estranged self
Scattered in each corner of the world

Seeds of my cells take root
Divided into one
This madness has become
My sanity, my every sense

Storms of intense emotions
Mirror my true image
Drifted on high and low tides
In love or in loneliness
I stretch my hands reaching out

Essama Chiba

Homonyms of Love

She is light,
Not heavy
And brilliant, too.

She is light,
Warms my skin outside
Ignites the fire inside.

She is light,
Cheerful and
Easily borne.

She is a breeze,
Easy to abide with
And fills my sails.

She is mine:
A place to seek what's precious
And belongs to me.

Allan Emery

My perfect vision

I have a charming vision,
A perfect dream to ease
My soul, giving a reason
To reap me piece by piece.

The common guy, as well
As the major decider,
Used to have the same spell,
Which grows wider and wider.

They used to hold their hands,
Forming a global chain,
And mused to stop the trends
To put the earth in vain.

It was that all the world
Was claiming, without cease,
The same and unique word,
In a giant chorus: "Peace!"

Ovidiu Cupsa

A Wasted Life

A man confused you shout against the world,
and hug the floor just like an infant curled.
It seems as though your life has flashed on by,
so sad the truth the waste just makes you cry.
The drink and drug abuse was all to blame,
with need, desire an incandescent flame.
That burned within and kept you from the track,
another bum laid out upon the rack.
Though now all clean and dry mistakes you curse,
for really things could not be any worse.
No job, no cash, no children or a wife,
you now pursue an ageing lonely life.
So kind at heart appear you old and grey,
impatiently you wait the close of play.

Alistair Muir

Spice is Nice [Than Bauk form] Burmese

Can't sleep on mat
man needs kyat; trades
fields fat, small price.

Wife churns milk nice,
no plain rice- mills
sweet spice to please.

Soon comes a breeze
Look! Ru-peeees! On
their knees,they catch.

Colleen

My Vow

In the morning, if the sun refuses to shine,
I will be there to guide you through the darkness.

You .. the love of my life
In the many years
of being together, I have tested
your love again and again
if In darkness of night, you feel
lost, grasp on to me, I will be there.

It is for you, these words I pen,
to thank you, for being,
my lover
my friend
As sure as the season's change
our love changes with it,
I will be faithful to the promises made.

As you stand by my side, no matter
what obstacle is hurled our way,
you shower me with steadfast love,
each and every day.
We bonded right from the start,
you stirred emotions .. invisible
to the average guy.

How can I thank you for being my
partner in life .. you brighten my
days, heat up my nights, you are
my fantasy, my every heart's desire
I can only offer my trust, devotion,
and my undying love for all eternity.

This has been, and is my vow to you.

Carrie Mercedes Gogo

Anger of the Rose.

My eyes have seen the anger of the rose
those innocent soft petals tend to lie,
die, I hear them whisper as they close.

Their thorns are by dark nature demon bred
led willingly to blood lust without care
where on these foolish mortals slowly fed.

Weep not for beauty tainted through disesase
these roots are planted where the summoned sleep
deep places only Hades ever sees.

Blue rose you are but Satan's hidden jest
blessed through every death that you eschew
due only to these souls yet unconfessed.

My eyes have seen the anger of the rose
those innocent soft petals tend to lie
die, I hear them whisper as they close.

Barry Hopkins

..... *Mashed not Fried* .....

The French are staunch and upright,
and they have such bulbous lips,
What's that my love? I can't get past
the fact she has no hips.

O' come on now, I caught you out,
your eyes were on her arse,
and that is where my foot will go
I'll part your cheeks quite sparse.

Maree Maree my chickadee
your curvature's just fine;
you're all I need, O' yes indeed,
Maree I'm glad you're mine.

O' go on now, you struck a chord
don't stop with just one line;
you best beware, you're splitting hairs,
make sure that they are mine.

Maree my love I stand aghast,
as implications rise;
I'm partial to potatoes more,
than skinny poor French fries.....

William Rout

Autumn by the Pond

I lie, dreaming morning to sleep
although Autumn on the Range
brings clouds piled from the east
and winds buffet tall eucalypts.

I watch eight delicate wings, fragile
as gauze, fracture the sun, shimmer
in gold, violet, bronze—splinter in
this curious ballet... Look!

Tracings on still water ghost their
crookedness, up-and-down hovers
of a mating flight jerking, and they write
'Survival of Dragonflies' like a plane

writes love letters in the sky but who
would deny their coupling, airborne blue
slenderness together between showers?

Mere wings whisper: 'Follow freedom'—
until winter freezes in!

Ron Wiseman

A Granite Goliath's PTSD

As colossal
as the gargantuan sentry Goliath,
he grows defiant before me
in Florence
with glaring eyes
turned toward Rome.

Gentle, pale faced pascal lamb,
but unlike past depictions
he bandstands as a giant alone,
the beauty of boyhood
with balls and backbone
of any man or woman.

I feel his singular moment
as a chiseled thought,
a ding-a-ling in his head.

He equivicates
between choice and action,
to put down his pen
and lift up a slingshot
to fight the inevitability,
a brazen fledgling engulfed in fate.

His stance in the arena,
a statue of Renaissance heroic,
I see ancient dead marble restored
as everyman's evocation of liberty.

His brow draws strength
from his daring spirit,
but I feel the tremors
and bulging veins of a right hand
taking command of an audience
in awe of huge exacting proportions.

Yet, it's his invisible inner iron ideals
as a Frankenstein of humanity
rising to heaven's height
that brings Michelangelo's David
to a final resting place
to sanction his silent legacy.

I listen in a courtyard
of alabaster white
for prayers;
he suffers pains from contemplating killing
and speaks psalms of repentance.

Laurie F. Grommett

Early Morning

White clouds were clean, pure as sheep new shorn
by clear creeks, sweetly slept through dawn;
silently, soft noises crept
as one by one each leapt
awake, to be seen
in meadows green
like posies
in high
sky!

Ron Wiseman

Listening to Her in Nature

I look into her many light brown golden strands of hay
She covers the land with many shimmering threads
that stretch out towards
the sun
I stop. And listen...listen
I deeply breathe in her warm earthy fragrance...

She is whispering to me...
"I want you, I want you
Fall into me now. I am so open to you
Fall into my thousands of arms and fingers delicately beckoning

Lie on me...in me
Let me envelop you my darling one
Let me take you inside me to the warm caring sensuous soul
that floats into
the earth
I need you
Now it is your time

My thousands of arms are all whispering with delight
fall fall fall"

So slowly and completely I fall intertwining golden threads

Divine...Divine...Divine

Stephen Hollins

Breakfast Alone

the morning tops
of cherry trees
burn

encoded messages
from the east

flicker images of your face
swim across
sleep sick eyelids

The hum of the fridge
deepens the silence
of an empty kitchen

at the sink
a blue china cup
and single silver spoon.

Dave Kavanagh

beyond our reach

we see beyond the sky
through atmospheric aberrations
dizzy into the vertigo of our ever expanding heavens
where iconic echoes of stars past still lit with magic
once thought to be gods now ghosts
in silence remind us of our own mortality

-jOsHua joSepH bIssoT -al art(0+)

...I Am...

Who am I, I heave a sigh,
and delve in deepest thought;
'tis something that I've asked myself,
'tis something that I ought.

I am me, it's all I see,
when gazing 'pon this glass,
I'm all I am, but with this pen
I add a little class.

I'm love to share with whom is there,
I let it freely flow,
'tis nurturing I love to give,
to help all others glow.

I'm humour that can turn a frown,
to smiles an ocean wide,
'tis laughter that does cleanse the soul,
and free it from inside.

I'm 'Daddio' O'don't you know,
I'm 'Hun' to my good wife,
I'm 'Diddily' when it's in jest,
those kids are so my life.

I'm patience at a steady pace,
but often times I fall,
I'm lover to my darling wife,
my God she makes me tall.

I'm a tradie who has worked his life,
with callous's on both knees,
to try to scribe a better life,
for those I love and need.

I'm 'Will' to you who read these lines,
a poet from afar,
you're all my kin in spirit true,
I have no avatar......

William Rout

Serenity Of Blue

Stir not my child, as ocean waits
serenity of blue
sleep deeply in my comfort
in dreams of softest hue.

My gentle touch of caring waves
will comfort you this night
as lands of dream you wander
enrobed in sparkled white.

Tomorrow waits with skies anew
on golden sand you lie
in caring arms of Morpheus
your sleep time lullaby.

No harm shall fall, in darkened touch
sweet child as soft you sleep
in harmony with ocean
and secrets from the deep.

Barry Hopkins

a slow death of the imagination

because

And-

just like that,
syllables fall asleep,
mottled synapses
strangle; suffocate

time lives in bottles
on top shelves of
neighbor's cabinets
who are never home,

there is no
place called home;
home is a diary page
torn from the inside

with ink blot stains
of when things
just were-

were different,
not today,
where everything
is, well-

missing

yesterday

missing,

a game
of hide and seek,

until she lies
under shattered
stained glass,

watches a cardinal,
tries to see
her reflection
through colored windows
and knows her life
outlived her mind

no one listens
to her thoughts

as if she were
born with broken limbs,
lacked a brain
or worse,
her heart

is

each vanished memory,
a billboard blinking
insanity;
an ice sculpture melting

time unwinds her
she tok ticks, tok ticks,
plays with legos, when once
she designed buildings

a shell of self
at nursery school,
peanut butter and fear
served for lunch

gone

no happy ending-

she's missed most
when one sits
next to her

when her daughter
is her mother,
the unknown shadow
in the corner, her son,

and she can't remember
what it is she's lost

crumbs.of.sorts.

Double Rainbow

Your love's so nice,
you've blessed me twice,
and on and on it goes
I give the world,
my birthday girl,
wrapped in a giant rose.

Your love's so deft,
all problems left,
there are none.
I'll love you always,
forever and all days,
and then some.

Allan Emery

Build A Pyre (For Orlando .....)

Sunshine peeks out from between
clouds floating languidly overhead

sectioning off bits of blue skies,
I wake to
nightmare storms
just finishing in the south,

pale still faces
reeling in horror
strange loud shouts explosions
blood spits out in all directions

--his beautiful face fiery
eyes very bravely
took up residence in
the one bedroom several
floored house hidden deep inside your heart:
breaking shattering wet on the floor--

fifty ghosts shoot off through
the ceiling praying baptising
giving first communion to whole populations,

a great river streams
from their mouths;

composed of melted weaponry
our smoking burning hatreds.

Cp Culliton

in.carnation (Falconnet #1)

When Leonardo wet a brand-new brush
or Edgar penned a line of poetry,
I wonder if they felt a kindred rush
to mine when I exalt my muse though she
represses every effort to bemoan.
Through lenses of the pinkest, brightest rose,
I see her hang a painting on her own,
ironic laughter pouring from my nose.
Imagine Mona Lisa on her farm—
a portrait here, a carpet made of fleece,
the decorations might reflect her charm
but all the while was SHE the masterpiece!

Her raven eyes are waiting for the night
with ten "pink elephants" in single file
...though not a muddy footprint in my sight.
(She walks intoxicatingly in style.)
I picture Poe's beloved lost Lenore—
when tears and cognac blended with the ink
and his sobriety was nevermore,
was SHE the spirit or was it the drink?

I recognize my wretched circumstance:
a boy with apples for the teacher's desk.
She elevates my heart and makes it prance,
but trembles as it trips the light grotesque.
Like ballerinas bend the arabesque
at Balanchine's academy in France,
is she— in costumes pink and picturesque—
the music or the reason that I dance?

The camera of my mind is at the brink...
my memory, a cubby hole to store
emotions when my soul was in the pink.
When Edie Sedgwick toured the Factory floor,
the clamor and commotion of the aisle—
her mouth, demure but full of dynamite,

and Warhol snapped the shutter, saying "Smile!",
was she the subject or the flash of light?

The answers to these questions lie in Greece
before the Milo Venus suffered harm.
The model (maybe someone's neighbor, niece,
whomever) had the beauty to disarm
yet still the *willingness* to strike a pose.
For she was both the statue AND the stone—
the form to flaunt, the courage to disclose.
My muse is discontent that she's alone,
no matter how well-meaning might I be,
how sweet the limelight or how pink the blush.
I fear the day I have to set her free
so she can be a better lover's crush.

Kaleb Pier

*I wanted to create a new poem form, so I present the falconnet.
The stanzas are 12-8-8-8-12 in iambic pentameter. The rhyme
scheme is "abab cdcd" etc. all the way up to "klkl", then turns back
around on itself, going from "lklk" down to "baba".

Bones

Lack of intellect
leaves me in a desert, parched,
searching grains for morning dew.

Finding only bones
my swollen tongue feels heavy,
words dry as salt on cracked lips.

Barry Hopkins

Vivaldi days

translucent ferns sketch January's pane
a dormant hush, a mute of feathered dawn
sly periscopic blades in search of spring
through virgin's crystal sea of frozen yawns

arthritic limbs and twig of exposé
sap phantom's intermission from the bark
warming wombs to waken bud and leaf
in filaments of gold from naked grief

a fertility of flowers all deflowered
their bridal petals drifting fragrant sighs
the furrowed fields have softened frowning brows
to Swallow encore flights from distant skies

Hallelujah angel's of first light
ovation's verdant canopies of shade
wings dance iridescence face to face
seduction's shortened garment of the night

tides glitter like a giggle on the beach
summertime bares castles on the sand
autumn peeps her wild emblazoned head
around the groaning labour of the land

storms arise to wash the canvas clean
winds sweep a dust of death as mould decays
earth opens up to feast on littered leaves
and sips the sweetest essence of belief

Ann Gilchrist

Missing Black and White Keys

Like a wisp in cold night
your warm breath...
drew camphor lines on breeze
before disappearing gradually
into the smokeless dawn.

Remembering that snowy day
fingers raining on that piano
and mine, strumming the guitar.

Lyrics spilled over walls
and songs grazing curtains
but, the notes were losing edge
lying haphazardly in dark corners.

The music died in footsteps
receding back to a world
never to be visited by voices
that knew the whispers
we can never put back...?
perhaps..but, I wish it would
ring..again.

Arjita Gupta

I'm Not Famous

Minnehaha, Lady Gaga
Monroe and James Dean,
famous faces, thoughts and places
things that might have been,
I'm not famous, only nameless
living in between.

Barry Hopkins

Learning to Fly

You come so close then pull away, it's so hard to see
through all the camouflage you put between you and me.
We're both coming from a history of heartbreak and pain,
determined we won't make those same mistakes again.

So how do we react when faced with our darkest fears?
Somehow we have to erase the intervening years,
that taught us all the wrong things, the wrong ways,
the way love's not supposed to be, we have to turn the page.

Open up a new chapter, start everything brand new,
remember this is today, not yesterday, avoid the rear view.
Just look ahead, the future is calling out to you,
and if I look I can see it's calling to me, too.

There's no changing the past, that has come and gone,
but we should change the future, we've waited for so long.
The steps are slow and painful, just take them one at a time,
together or apart we have to know, everything will be fine.

I come so close then pull away, it's hard to make the change,
but I'm willing to give it a try, learn to adapt and rearrange
my old ways of thinking that kept me on the ground,
it's a different day, a different world; I'm learning to fly now.

Michele Wass

..... *Besotten Ways*.....

Besotten 'midst a tendresse drop of effervescent green,
his love for her found endless means and manner to be seen.
She bore the horticulture mark of one who tends the Earth,
her love and tender caring ways by trees she was agirt.

He loved her once amidst the blooms of daffodils in spring,
her heart was his upon the reading of the verse he brings.
She is the one who tends the plants for beauty to be seen,
and he the poet of the words that bring the page agleam.

Together they are both besoothed by one another's ways,
with love so grand a marriage sealed them 'till their dying days.
If she passed first he'd be besoothed 'midst effervescent trees,
If he passed first she'd have his words to sooth her tendresse needs.

Together once their curtain draws and both have passed afree,
she'll find him writing words of love, for her under God's trees.....

William Rout

water stands still

the arc of dawn
rushes the tide of day
and the morning burns
even under the palo verde

no rest
from a million mindful pulls
racing against
a hundred needful things to be done

the afternoon's a blur

until with horse and rope
chasing steer against the clock
i ride easy into the box
to call for my steer

prairie dust ceases
it's dance

as mocking birds
dirty kids and barking dogs
passing trains pulling boxcars
filled full of life's concerns

disappear

water stands still
and i in the vortex
of time's peace

ride and rope

unfettered
once more
Jamesvm

blocked call?

she wasn't five or twenty-five
when she found herself
more than sad.

it rings;
incessant screeching digits,

before hello,
vibrations pierce.

well versed
in phone language
her hands understand,

"why,
how come, I'm your mother,
you should."

and...
why should she do anything
anyway,

child tucked under her shirt
husband groping,

'I don't have to...
I have a degree,
I can think
for myself.'

grownups get to make their own rules

isn't that why five-year-olds
are in a hurry to get 'grown'?

she realizes
five-year-olds
do not know hard plastic
has a law degree,

sentences daughters
to a lifetime
of hard labor

five-year-olds
do not know
old people
are five-year-olds
with grey hair
wrinkles, and
a need for sandboxes.

growing up
does not mean much,
no matter one's age
a child remains,

she waits,
wants,
hopes...

for an acceptance letter
today,
tomorrow,
instead comes
an IOU

from the one
who birthed her,

a laundry list
of conditional love.

"but….."

"but what?"

"grow up."
(mother wants to be her friend)
"I wish you were more like…"

to which she will say,
"I might be
if you were…"

shockwaves continue,
pulse through her palms,
another follicle dies.

"I wish you were different".

she can not reply,
electricity paralyzes
her hand,
stops her heart.

she will never
be enough
which just may be why,

she finds herself sad

crumbs.of.sorts.

Connections

A flea above the marble while
the ocean ebbs and flows,
I ponder as the cumulus
is foam between my toes.

They say, "Another fish will come
and lo! the sea is vast.
Your patience will be justified,
the pleasure unsurpassed."

They add, "It makes no common sense
to hum a somber hymn
and if you truly care for her,
you have to let her swim."

They tell me, "When you least expect,
a trophy takes the bait
without a hook, without a line;
you simply need to wait."

In truth, my wasted, paper heart
had sailed a shred too high,
but like the sun for Icarus,
she made me want to fly.

Poetic wax had melted fast
and thus the deathly knell.
My only indication was
a backward fare-thee-well.

I question if we ever were
on equal, level planes—
if, when it didn't work, that she
felt corresponding pains.

The past has passed. It doesn't help

to pout and reminisce,

but is it so unorthodox
if she's the one I miss?

Another destination looms
as both of us explore
though cloudy skies' uncertainty
lends little to rapport.

I wonder when she's seen the world,
if left to her device,
conceivably that she could jump
inside the same boat twice.

Kaleb Pier

Very, Very Cruel

She is just seventeen,
beginning to understand her powers.
Yet, she will, she must, subject herself
to a cold, calculating knife:

"We must remove the tumor first,"
the surgeon remarks, kindly,
"and then we will know more surely if the breast... "

The girl thinks back to yesterday, remembers his words,
sees that the pizza she nibbles is growing greasy and cold;
her finger-tips are cold, too, as she nervously fondles
her beryl brooch and her eyes, tragically, mistily tell her,
beyond any reproach, that life is suddenly strange
and very, very cruel and seemingly forbidding and old.

Ron Wiseman

Neighbours

Love them or hate them, they're there every day
living next door and won't go away
neighbours we call them, yours, maybe mine
hate them, it's trouble, love them it's fine.

Maybe they're noisy with horrible kids
running like sauceans with ill-fitting lids
sometimes with pets, kittens and dogs
or something exotic like poisonous frogs.

Above and below if you live in a flat
or maybe a house and a snarling black cat
maybe they're noisy, maybe they're nice
some maybe friends with lots of advice.

Should they be vampires, then what the heck
wake up one morning, they're biting your neck
maybe they're sexy, the love of your life
maybe your neighbour could be your next wife.

Barry Hopkins

The Poetess

The poetess heard from her beau
"You're made like a poet, you know?"
You've got Longfellow's feets,
got Anne Brontë's teats,
and an ass like Maya Angelou!

Allan Emery

Maya Angelou was a nightclub dancer for a time and was said to
have quite a nice figure. I think this was intended as a compliment.

Moving

Of our last days,
each,
I've packed a piece.

Yesterday
is kept.
Sorrows wept,
for with
these boxes
my heart
has left.

You,
my body
will not forget.
Lies were just
as real,
as love.

This mind
smiles for
the truth.
I must now bring
my body
to the man of
my heart.

Hope dies,
and elsewhere
it is reborn.
Yet still Robby,
the memories
will live on.

Alison Emery

behind every beautiful thing

Every September for twelve years she wore ponytails and used milk
money to purchase sanguine moments as school bells rang
signaling summer stargazing was over.

Each dream, recorded with peacock blue ink folded in notebooks of
pink colored paper, watched oxford shirts that failed to foreshadow
endings which were starched in hidden pockets so hope could
continue to walk in saddle shoes or loafers, blind to pennies about
to fade; seasons passed before she swept bangs of war-torn todays
from her face, cut her ponytails short, allowing her to twirl fear like
a curly-cue on top of a melting ice cream cone.

Then, the ice man came, he brought with him, the silence of silent
sounds screaming; her God forgot to say goodbye, she held a flag
meant to honor and blanketed herself goodnight.

crumbs.of.sorts.

On Building Walls

We build our walls to keep them out,
we build to seal us in,
believing if they're high enough,
we'll be the ones to win.
But nothing's healed and nothing's won
when minds are far apart,
the bricks just keep us out of touch,
at a distance from our heart.
Where we don't have to see or talk,
reach out or try to mend,
they'll always be our enemy,
they'll never be our friend.

Where communication is lost
wounds fester and they rot.
We're separate now, but far from safe,
you see, that's just what we got,
when first we stacked
those stones to reach the sky.
It's not a world of peace we built,
that's just an artful lie
they told us to convince us
what they said was right,
but walls don't keep us safe,
they just block out the light.

Michele Wass

Tiger Moth

The double-engine darts across the dusk,
oblivious to obstacles ahead.
Precipitation pelts the wooden husk,
so hail the pilot, brave and battle-bred.
His thin propellers hum a rasping tune,
providing only moments left to fly.
The sun is horizontal and will soon
have sunk for good behind the silver sky.
As darkness fast approaches, should he yield
and turn around to search for fresher light?
His scars are old, but deeper wounds have healed;
it simply never happens overnight.
No sadder soldier under fruitless aim:
a moth attracted to a dying flame.

Kaleb Pier

Sun Flower

Even though she blew in the wind
she elected not to break, just bend,
not give way when the sun beat down,
never let it beat her into the ground,
even when the heat made her weep
she let the tears water her deep.
And everyday she grew stronger,
each assault fortifying her armor
until the day she felt her petals unfurl,
and she radiated light into the world.

Michele Wass

It's a Thingummy.

Do I suck it, do I blow it ?
Can I pick it up and throw it
I don't know what it is or where its been.

Can I drink it, can I eat it ?
Tell me, would you like to meet it
can I paint it in a subtle shade of green.

I know it's not a lion
it hasn't got a tie on
I'm sorry but I haven't got a clue.

I don't think its my brother
cos he looks like my mother
would I find one if I typed it in Yahoo ?

It's an elephant, it told me
it picked me up and rolled me
I like it, can have it for a pet ?

I'll keep it in my bedroom
it needs a lot of headroom
excuse me while I go and find a vet.

Barry Hopkins

Smile Please.

Point this camera, point it well
oh what stories it might tell.
Make them smile, make them frown
just don't use it upside down !

Barry Hopkins

faded laughter~

I stand
among white billows,
watching poles collapse,
clouds fall.

I see
a worn painted smile
turn blue
on a mask, still alive
with vibrant colored memories
of my childhood,

you-
collector of colorful
cotton-candy moments,
the one who dared me
to teeter and fall
provided a safety net
of outstretched arms

threads unravel-

washed in alcohol baths
and oxygen
my smile fades

I wonder,
'can my show can go on?'

my tragic clown
intuits fears,
expels
a father's love-

one large breath
into a balloon

labeled
'for daughter'-

begs me,
'take it,'
his last bow,
an almost inaudible whisper:

"it's your show now, kid,
today I'm going to die."

fifty glass clowns weep,
they try to rhyme in frowns
a verse that begs you
'live.'

too late

my circus hobo
is packed,
ready to move on
pretends for me,
to laugh,

begins to die-

I-
pretend you'll live.

crumbs.of.sorts.

The Proof

Because of her, my heart is like the moon
and hovers in the heavens, giving light
to liberate her from a lonely June.
My wish is that she may (or that she might)
be sheltered in my shining love tonight.
The distance that we douse with our disdain
will dissipate the day we reunite.
I wax pathetic, though 'tis all in vain;
her lunar loyalty begins to wane.
Our phase was full but since has dimmed to dark.
She claims the harmony is now mundane,
but fails to see the moonlight for the spark.
To you who reads: when love is less than grand,
the proof is in the putting up a stand.

Kaleb Pier

I love apples

for chewing
and cider sipping;
for sayings like
"She's apples!"

I had a lady teacher
seventy years ago
and I was the apple
of her eye, I think.

Mind you, Eve
was the apple
of Adam's eye!

Ron Wiseman

Little diamond

From which kingdom eternal,
oh my grand son, is your arrival!
I am so fond of your sweet smile
that I look for it all the while.

I like you weep with folded lip,
you appear naughty at its top;
In crying also you are wonderful
I praise God and become thankful.

I remember one video vividly
you were drinking milk gladly,
lying on your mother's lap
while father was taking a snap.

You look so beautiful
while sitting inside dad's lap-hole,
dad being quite tall
and you are so small!

Your grand-mom is so dear
you enjoy all fun with her;
we eagerly wait for the funfair
as your rice-eating ceremony is coming near.

Sandip Saha freelance writer

carbon paper

I wrote between lifelines,
myself, a life

filled in decayed spaces
which embedded themselves
in mother's tongue,

landed in classrooms,
that sent home report cards
forged in grades, so-

another semester

I will not be chained
to a kitchen chair, alone,
to eat cold cheese sandwiches
trying not to choke down
thick slices of yellow self-esteem

while all other children play outside

crumbs.of.sorts.

a snowflake's story

encased in an insulated bubble
sealed from a colorless world outside.
she sees through diaphanous veils of wonderment,
watches snowflakes tumble
inside her white-washed world of safe-
until clouds from a shattered sky
ribbon through outstretched arms,
lie laced with dreams strewn somewhere,
yearning,
yearning,
to be found

crumbs.of.sorts.

Sky Light

A hunger sits inside my mouth,
but I can not taste morning flavor on its tongue.
My ears crave your words, remembering.
The butterflies have lost their way through dawning light.

Laurie F. Grommett

a subject without a verb

she woke,
nothing was-

her ground, black

still, she reached
for remembrances
of stars
and wept for yesterday
when she never rained

craving to relive
the moon's wink
her fingertips
interpreted the sky
like a braille sonnet,

was a time midnight
came at midnight
and sunshine followed dawn

she prayed for her star,
as charcoal fell
between her fingers-
and shut out the noise

the moon mourned-

caressed a photograph
of his little girl-

she was swinging

from his cusp
as he brushed stars
in her eyes

she gave them away—

crumbs.of.sorts.

To Dream of You

As I arrange my tousled curls upon a silken rest,
to dream of you so tranquil with your head upon my breast.
I lie beside you naked that your eyes alone may see,
this woman who you say you love, the secret core of me.

I am no longer young my darling, neither am I old,
the fires of love still burn and they keep me from the cold.
While flushed I am with passion for reasons you bestow,
as here we lie as lovers, flesh aflame in afterglow.

I dream of you at sunrise and when the evening's cold,
when forest leaves are lush and green or autumn, turning gold.
My dreams are now but moments, just grains of granuled sand,
as on the tide they ebb and flow I seek to kiss your hand.

I come to you my darling with naught but joyous love,
as tenderly you cherish me 'neath velvet skies above.
To hear you say you love me and I am your Faberge,
brings tears of such sweet happiness with dreams of you this day.

Lulu Gee

Dreamer's Portal

Standing, marking disembarking,
threshold to a dreamer's view,
arguments and rude remarking,
elbowing in narrow parking
fade to mists of yester-you.

Barely more than post and lentil,
frame askew with wind-worn door.
Lacking paint and ornamental,
egg and dart are incidental
to what draws me to your core.

Peaks of purpose lie extending,
luminosity set free.
Hours wasted need upending,
through my portal soar, ascending
barriers to majesty.

Feel the mountain breezes flourish
through the meadow's floral crown.
Breathe the air, it's there to nourish,
let your actions be more Muir-ish,
ride the lift of zephyr's down.

Mark Andrew James Terry

The Tracks of My Years

I feel like a crosstie beneath rusted rail,
awaiting a weight that will never return.
The years that I prospered are fall's early burn
and winter reminds me I'm fragile and frail,
unable to earn, a seasonal tale.

Technology passing is blurring my view,
no longer familiar are terms being used.
The content and factions have left me confused,
and ethics seem bygone like Steamliner's crew,
their service excused with nothing to do.

The young bucks are gloating, they're bloated with pride,
with gadgets for problems, analytical slide.
They know less of beauty and how it's applied,
they're there for the ride, commitment untied.

Mark Andrew James Terry

Swag of Reave — A Triolet

Those high-born feathered nests, I'm told,
are desolate. Though that's naive,
they're brimming with a full billfold,
those high-born feathered nests. I'm told
they're suited to survive the cold
with interwoven swag of reave.
Those high-born feathered nests, I'm told,
are desolate, though that's naive.

Mark Andrew James Terry

The Rise of Rose

Come see the rise of rose on morning seas
when newborn days blend teal to tangerine;
when tawny grays decrease by small degrees,
transforming tidal pools from bland to green.
Come taste a salt divine within the air,
and quiver senses, peel away the stress.
Enrobe in joie de vivre with laissez faire,
appreciating nature's sweet finesse.
Tomorrow's problems evanesce like fog;
cerebral mists give way to clarity.
That sun, you see, is nooning over Prague
enlivening the verve of verity,
and hours swimming monetary streams
can ne'er return, except within your dreams.

Mark Andrew James Terry

Poems fell apart

Some threw themselves down the window
Some shot themselves in the mouth
Some threw their hands on a blade
And the rest
Reincarnated into a woman
Who walks every single day of autumn
-with a flower pot in her hands-
In search for a man
who blossomed in the winter
and shed leaves in the spring

Sept Matin

The Completed Puzzle

Yes Dear!
On earth
you are my Boulder,
and through the Universe
you are my Quasar!

Yes Dear!
It is you,
your love,
your strength
that is in every way,
a completion
to the puzzle of my life!

Yes Dear!
You are the sediment
for my strength,
it is you
your illumination
which is the light -
my full moon!

Yes, my Dear Love,
Your arms are the walls
That encase me home.
That keep me snug.

Yes Dear!
Your forever home
And all of your pearls
are inside of my heart!

Alison Emery

Moments Tides Expel

that summer's heat desired you,
your hue an urn to idolize,
its auburn bronzing simmering
with sun and sea salt shimmering
on skin that harbored eyes.

untangled ringlets wet with gold
would sway a way to mesmerize
and as you moved your silhouette
would cause the core of want to whet,
a compliment to August skies.

within your eyes were silver beams
the moon and stars had given you.
they understood that secrets kept
are pools of dreams that lovers wept,
there you and I would woo.

but summer burned my memory,
then autumn passed and so did love
as decades grew a thorny wood
o how I'd go back if I could
to hear the coo of passion's dove.

my breath is just a whisper now
and soon I'll be a broken shell
but even shells have lives once lived
where sunsets courted, love was sieved
from moments tides expel.

Mark Andrew James Terry

Shallow Depth

Sometime I watch them staring,
bemocking, mumbling as they
pass you by with clueless grins
revealing that their only depth lies below
in the sludge beneath their shoes -
so, how could they possibly know…

it's your depth that keeps you silent,
while filled with wisdom that if spoken
would send their small minds
spinning into the stratosphere,
as every intelligent thought orbited
around you and slowly disappeared.

How could anyone comprehend -
you are a universe, a fulgid force
with eyes set ablaze by mysteries
from the suns brilliant burn,
and that volumes lie undisclosed
within your sweet enigmatic smile.

How could they know?

skkingrey

Broken out

I wasn't grown enough
To bear the pain
Which life was ready to give me.

I wasn't make up my mind
To understand
what is happening that time.

I wasn't hard hearten
To be strong
When i was in a situation to see that.

The beating of my heart was so violent and wild
that I felt as if my life were breaking from me

Everything around me turned dark
and
I sat idle with tears

Broken out in to pieces
When I came into conscious.

I saw a beautiful idol
Lying before me idle.

I see no smile,
On her rosy lips.
I see no curls of hair,
Floating in air.
I can't hear a word,
from her .
When I hug her,
She was cold.

I understood
She went into deep sleep.
I understood

She will never speak to me.
I understood
I can't be with her anymore.

The beating of my heart was so violent and wild ,
that I felt as if my life were breaking from me .
Broken out in my life,
For the first time.
Yet my soul is dying for her,
whenever I think her.

Kiruthika Karthik

Georgia Heat

Between Ohio and the Georgia heat
where smoke around a restless crowd appears,
a woman grips her heart to feel the beat
and breathes the mirthful music through her ears.
In silence, she is prone to suffocate
but ample oxygen is found in song.
The lights onstage that serve to incubate
will cause her soul to hatch before too long
and ligaments that link her aching bones
(which carry carefully the weight of life)
are struck and buckled by the bass's tones,
but she is steadfast in the face of strife.
The drummer kicks to lift another curse—
her blood is blessed to travel in reverse.

Kaleb Pier

There Is Always a Man

Dragonflies began
Their life span
When a woman
Shaved her hair
Mourning a soldier
Who had never existed

The men who have never existed
Set off for the battle
before every other man sets,
And point their guns
before every other soldier intents,
And fall dead on the ground
before every other woman forgets
There was always a man;
she loved.

Sept Matin

What Makes a Man a Man

Y

…because x was just not enough

Mark Andrew James Terry

The Magic Forest

Oh, what magic in this forest
Where moonbeams gently fall,
Where jade blue pines are numinous
When night time comes to call.
And stars silver and glistening
At play with leaf and fern,
While snowy owls drift on the breeze
With anything nocturne.
I hear the crickets plaintive tune
As bats skim overhead,
While noises from the undergrowth
Are filling me with dread.
Between the trembling hanging vines,
I sense I'm almost there,
I've crept here once or twice before -
In wonderment to stare.

For here I see the fairy mound
Deep in the sheltered grove,
I'm blinded by the mystic light,
Where all shines misty mauve.
These nymphs I spy in petal gowns
With arms like buttermilk,
Begin to dance and murmur songs
In voices soft as silk.
At night when everything is still
These fairies are not shy,
They dance when dark and rarely sleep,
While days go softly by.
And high above the naked moon,
The stars look down with charm
And should you see these laughing nymphs,
Then you'll be free from harm.

Lulu Gee

Oh Maggie

Greenest grasses' wetted growing,
sweetest clover inflorescence
lie in pastures that are flowing
with some blackbirds' chattered crowing,
recollection of an essence.

There is music that transports me
to my first untested passion,
when a horse was friend and trustee;
when the girls were warm and busty,
and my heart was plum not ashen.

In a saddle on that ranch road,
in the bower of my life's load
lives the flower of my being
where the morning hues are gleeing
and the reaper's scythe not owed.

Oh Magnolia how I love thee
with your silken petals basking,
where the stream of living flows free
and the joy of new discov'ry
is the song of youth's unmasking.

Oh my Maggie how I love thee
and you're still abloom within me.

Mark Andrew James Terry

Keeper

You've been my greatest dream,
and to lose you has been my biggest fear.
But to love you has been my greatest adventure♥.

Madison Wakefield

With your Memories

I didn't know you wanted to be with me.
I didn't know you wanted to feed me food.
I didn't know you wanted to sing a lullaby for me.
I didn't know you wanted to dress up me
and put a beautiful plait.
I didn't know you wanted me to be the first
in studies, sports and more.
I didn't know you wanted me to become a best person.
I didn't know you always think about me,
though you were not with me.

But
I don't know these, because I was little that time

I know you faced a plenty of troubles for me,
I know you felt very sad when I wear a spectacles ,
I know you love me more.

Mom, this is not fair,
When I come to know ,
How much you want me to be with you,
You left me,
You left me to a distant place,
where I cant even come now.

I am here how you like!
Good in studies,
Good in sports,
Even good in cooking,
Good at my office too.

Winning more awards,
Winning more medals,
People praise me, you are best at this and that.
I want you too know these,
So you will be happy about me.

Only
With your memories,
I am trying to survive.
Hiding all my feel for you,
Within myself.
I love you more

Kiruthika Karthik

Sonnet For The Many

Who will write for mass of many
tasking for the righteous penny?
Who will cry their anguished hours
toiling in those tower bowers?
Who will pen for them, if any;
who will fight for shackle freeing?

All the seven billion beings
feeling, hearing, tasting, seeing,
smelling draft of riches passing
knowing that they're not amassing
bare-enough for guaranteeing
even final flowers.

Who will write for mass of many,
all the seven billion beings?

Mark Andrew James Terry

Old Hell's Bay

Its muck, a mired mangled mead,
lies quietly 'neath frond and reed
and teems un-wrangled wriggled rank,
while misting settles dark and dank
and nettles web's wet bead.

Primordial is Old Hell's Bay,
where snakes and owls seek their prey.
The slithering slip silently
and strike to kill so violently
but fear the raptor's flay.

An arch of feathered-needles green
the edges of this ancient scene.
Its wooded grey is fey and still
and sinks to lay without a hill...
for some it's nature's mean,

but I see life's vivacity
within the rise of cypress tree,
in spanish moss that tangles there
and dappled light, and tonic air
that ripples tannin sea.

Through sphagnum mazes minnows race
and polliwogs join riot's chase,
above them tightly gripping bark
the impish squirrels leap and lark,
traversing crown to base.

All small stand tall within the swamp
as tiny orchids own their pomp,
mosquitoes buzz and gather swarm
to seek out blood from something warm
when herds of white-tail romp,

and even there where water reigns

are knolls that yellow-pine wood gains
a hold to bower sow with shoat,
and possums with their joeys tote
afar away from highway lanes.

A panther cries an angry growl
and gator lurks with ghastly scowl,
while bobcats slink a lynx's prowl
past feral hog with tusk in jowl.
A treasure-trove of life exists
within the secret turns and twists
of wood-eternal's cowl.

Mark Andrew James Terry

Demons in my mind

When I turn my head to assess behind
and to give myself surer peace of mind,
anyone can see that I'm paranoid
and the demons there are not anthropoid,
rather wisps of fear of imagined kind.

Those beleaguered thoughts are without reprieve
bringing imagery that I misconceive,
and they vie for space in between each breath
setting apprehension of even death,
a foreshadowing that the truth deceives.

And I kid myself no one else can see
that I'm terrified that they're after me.

Mark Andrew James Terry

The Breath of Death

To all, I say beware...
when tides inform the autumn seas
that shadows fear the were-banshees,
the coven comes to call The Beast
and too, the spirits long deceased
to be its devotees.

It wasn't from beneath the waves,
where lie the bones of lord and slaves,
or on the hill above the dunes,
that holds the stones with ancient runes
inscribed on troubled graves,

but from the swirls within the mist
in light of night where eyes insist
that shadowed movement comes to seek
the ones in fright, whose knees were weak,
each seeking demon's list.

Brave terror lurked within our mind,
it festered there, became entwined,
entangled by the slightest sense
with nerves impaired by chilled suspense
at what the night might find.

Emblazoned moon rose o'er the beach,
a celebrant, as to beseech
the coven's few who through that night
had offered chant by firelight,
the demon's ear to reach.

Their candles flicked though air was still.
As if a wounded bat's sad shrill,
their chanting called to fiendish host,
a sound attuned that's so engrossed
all present peace was nil.

Then, just at once each wick unlit
and chanting slowed as to emit
a tone unlike I've ever heard,
the darkness lowed and shadows stirred,
to wit, unholy writ.

My friend and I were yet unseen
within sea oats and goat's foot green
that vines along the edge of drift
where sand promotes its shape to shift
and crabs find dead to preen.

We felt the breath of ancient dew
ascend from some impious pew
and gather 'round in thickly stew
as coven drum beat evil cue...
alerted to we two.

As every eye bore through to us,
we saw The Beast and smelt its puss
that oozed and dripped onto our backs,
a fearing's feast description lacks
of sure death's incubus.

Without a word we rose and ran.
We ran as fast as humans can
and never once did turn to look
with eyes aghast as fearing shook
the growth of boy to man.

To all, I say beware...
When tides inform the autumn seas
that shadows fear the were-banshees,
the coven comes to call The Beast
and too, the spirits long deceased
to be its devotees.

Mark Andrew James Terry

Countless Sparrows

Five sparrows
Two sparrows
Seven sparrows
Eight sparrows
Six sparrows
Three sparrows

There was a young painter
Who would stare out the window
The whole mornings

Sept Matin

Reculver After the Storm

The sky is focused, crystal clear, so blue.
The shingles battered, like a giant stair!
Our dogs and me, who's arm in arm with you
stroll blissful on the beach without a care .

Roman towers pierce the brittle sky.
Ancient groynes deployed to turn the sea
now like the towers crumble, sit awry
like giants, who've become an amputee.

That sea that's never aged has calmed again
to blend with distant shorelines into haze,
while gentle horses troubled its terrain
today the sun has set this world ablaze.

a palette for the hallowed bell that chimes,
how fickle nature alters life sometimes.

Daniel Lake

Armageddon

Her eyes dripped cinnamon
onto the cold steel,
forming bubbles of emotion.

Blue she mused
or a heavy tint of red?

The day was not bloody enough for red
or expansive enough for blue.

She poondered, idly dawdling,
ethching battleship grey
into her indecisiveness.

Pretty, she purred,
just the effect of war torn scenery.

That was when she met him;
7 p.m. on the dot.

He knew immediately from her look
this was not the sort of day
to mess with her.

Barry Hopkins

On Reading a Faerie Tale

Those pages seemed to melt away
as words to view reformed
and posies grew on every grave
except for one inscribed with Knave
and 'round that ravens swarmed.

Their cawing raked at peacefulness
and fluttered feathers flew
but radiance from distant moons
encouraged me to seek raccoons
who lived beneath a pew.

They spoke in ancient Raccoonese
that somehow I could speak.
They whispered secrets to themselves
about the faeries and the elves
whose homes were near the creek.

I ventured there to ask of them
just how I came to be
a traveler in unknown land
and sought from them to understand
how they could be so wee.

But elves and faeries never tell
and with a tinkling of a bell
a-fast to sleep I fell.

Mark Andrew James Terry

The Greatest Desired Journey

What is a life,
But the sorrow
At a life's end?

To some life's like algebra.
To some life's like music.

What is birth
But the joy
Of a life's creation?

And everywhere in-between
Birth and death
Lies a multitude of paths.

What are days,
But a gift
Of gravity?

To fill in life's blank map
marks a treasure,
A greatest desired journey.

Alison Emery

The Scarecrow

The scarecrow stands in sad repose
alone, he waits in fading clothes
with sagging coat, a cotton shirt
that now are aged with mould and dirt.

His pipe lays broken on the ground,
his nose that late someone had found
and placed with glee below his cap;
My, how he looked a loathsome chap.

Remembering when he was born
that day, by children on the lawn
made lovingly, though his attire
like him, was destined for the fire.

His eyes when placed, so he could see
those children thrilled, who clapped with glee
who named him 'Guy' and gave him hair
but one small girl thought this unfair.

'Claire' looked at him with eyes steadfast
and told him she was just aghast.
'To burn you's wrong!' (so to this end)
she simply dared protect her friend.

She stood defiant, arms apart
(for Guy had somehow stole her heart)
and begged her parents, spare his fate,
(though other children were irate.)

Her daddy saw he had to yield
and carried them both to a field,
where now Guy stands, a forlorn plight
to guard the peas by day and night.

Alone he waits so glum, forlorn,
his clothes now rotting dirty, worn,

and dreams about his little friend
who spared him from a firey end.

So many years had seen poor Guy
disheveled, when Claire happened by
she stopped and saw her old scarecrow,
so far forgotten long ago.

How selfishly she'd left him here
and sadly as she wiped a tear,
she felt the urge to hug poor Guy
regretting leaving him to die.

Her tears as they fell on his chest
soon penetrated his old vest
and touched him deep, where life would start;
(The magic of a loving heart.)

The scarecrow blossomed, (stories can)
those tears changed Guy into a man.
Now young and strong he gently kissed
The girl he'd always loved and missed.

Yes fairy tales at times come true,
your love for him, his love for you
will prosper, just remember this,
'the magic of a tender kiss.'

The moral is be firm, be true.
Be resolute and stick like glue.
Just look beyond a sad, flawed face,
for love, is where we interlace.

Dan Lake

Karkinos of Cancer

United as the grains of sand
Zeta,tis time to claim your hand-
I, Karkinos, battlefield's victor-
survivor of Twelve Labors war

chewed Hercules' foot in deep mire
as he clinched nine-headed Hydra.
Super might of his Greecian thigh
debarred me from bidding goodbye.

Enraged, he kicked at claw of mine
compelled me high to skyward line.
Faithful Hera did not leave me
that I should die, as we can see.

This fated day live not alone
Oh crusty bride, no longer groan!
Darling, my heart hungers for more
to embrace you on ebbing shore.

Utter goodbye to earth's crater
join our constellation Cancer.
Claw-in-claw twinkling from above
Zeta, you'll be my stardom love.
Colleen Selvon-Rampersad
Precision

Sunlight steps out of
a grey mantle of raindrops;
she contemplates bees hopping
in Fibonacci spirals,
tiny physicists teaching Einstein
precision.

Deb Blondell-Pitt

Pulse 49

bitter dark
vicious venom
boomeranging loathe again

cruel return
bullets reign ing
fourty-nine lie still within

swollen graves
lined by shadows
trepidation torrents in

differences are beautiful,
bedouin and lesbian.
today's the day to re-begin
and think of love as not a sin.

when God when
will loving win?
when will loving win?

Mark Andrew James Terry

Just know, if you're going to Judge me …

I'm

not weird,

I'm delightfully

different.

Alison Emery

Two Wayward Dogs

i met you under a deluge of birdsong
fifty years ago
i think
for safe sex
often
or for love
i don't really know
but we were young
and i kissed
with my eyes
to open them
now
after a long
marriage
and I see wrinkles
graying hair
half-smiles and i'm
far too deaf
to hear your voice
spit out
if you still fancy me
being impotent
and all that

never now
two wayward dogs
locked alone
and hot with instinct

Ron Wiseman

Grief

Sometimes -
no matter
what you do
You can't wake up.
It's as if you've
gone to sleep
Yet sleep is wake
And wake is sleep.
It's much easier
for people to feel
Your pain as opposed
to your joy.

I have no business
deducting why,
Any more
than my business
Is to try
to be anything
other than human.
But I will tell you this,
Grief
is much more difficult
to forget
Than joy.

As it seems
joy always comes
second
to grief.
And that,
is the
moment
you wake up.

Alison Emery

Morning Glitter

You hang below the sky in contemplation,
guarding all below your sturdy boughs;
the Spanish Moss, a scrounging decoration,
waving under arms it soft endows.

The morning glitter frames your winsome glory,
flitting like a bee from leaf to leaf,
as enigmatic smiles impart a story
like some saucy fine aperitif .

Sweethearts pledged their fervour, 'neath your canopy.
Names engraved, remind us of their love.
Resting we can dream of loves sweet fantasy,
beneath your awe-inspiring jewels above.

We poets sit, our muses conjure passions;
thinking, 'twixt the glory nature's made.
Rewriting poems in the latest fashions
and dream of saffron soul-days in the shade.

Dan Lake

Silver Bird

Silver bird where do you go?
In the ghostliness of moonlight,
As you cut the dark sky
From five miles high
Into slices with vapour trails white.

Where have you come from today?
What lands have you crossed and what seas?
Have you crossed high mountains
And rococo fountains
Or white beaches, with tall palm tree's?

Did you look down on man made towers?
Where thousand will toil all day,
Or great reef's perhaps
Where man dives to relax
Or volcano's on islands that play.

Have you crossed the great deserts below,
Or the forests so deep and so wide,
Have you seen the canal
Where sails the whit dhow
Where no movement will come from the tide.

Where the heat from the sun is so hot
That it bleaches the bones of the dead,
Or the freezing pole waste
Where death ends in haste
Where man is so wary to tread.

Silver bird where have you been?
With your cargo that needed to roam,
They come back again
To the bus and the train
To this place where so many call home…

Dan Lake

Beauty n beast

Flower from flora
Wild from fauna
Sea, cloud on route to travel
Touch of kisses n pure love
Understanding life of creatures

Souls over souls in night
Some buried remains fossils
Some can't be touched nor seen
Just an intuition of senses of nature

Beauty n beast together in a slope of unity
Rain n sun makes sustainable forest
Lime, salty sea n breeds of animal's
For long a closed n open loop of connected

Like a green apple clouds full of taste
Beneath lap molten lava formed erupt
Exploiting its beauty in beast world.

Rnayak

The Fifteen Syllable Poem

I've set myself a quandary which at first was just a notion,
a simple fifteen syllable to set this rhyme in motion.
Not concerned nor overburdened, by the sheer enormity,
Of writing fifteen syllies in four line's of poetry .

You have noticed that I failed in that last poor repartee.
The final line in stanza one is wrong from this devotee.
But still I strive, I toil, contrive, to conquer this conundrum
This fifteen syllable is hard, I'm finding it quite humdrum.

Although I find this weariness, encompassing, inviting
In the early morning calmness; you'll find me dreaming, writing.
And though I might at last transcribe some semblance of my trial,
I think I'll ponder somewhere else; and leave this for a while…

Dan Lake

After Dew

Your parted crimson glistening
leaves cardinal imprints,
they blush of dew,
say, "I love you,"
with feral fingerprints.

No longer are you pressing in
to sew soft cambric knowing,
and in the quiet seep of night
I sense our evanescing light
and resonance is slowing.

Mark Andrew James Terry

..... *The Call of Zanzibar* .....

In elven lands a shimmering did tinker 'neath the shroud,
of autumn leaves and hollowed logs, a canopy so proud.
'Twas there a spritely elven gent cast mystery afar,
with elven song and quavered flute, the sounds of Zanzibar.

A cherished land of hidden charm and mystic overture,
where elves and fairies sprinkle dust of gold to be procured.
'Tis where the rainbow meets the Earth and leprechaun's are found,
a magic kingdom hidden midst the leaves upon the ground.

In Zanzibar the crystal waters ebb and flow so clear,
and wash upon the purest sand, a sight to hold so dear.
'Tis where the mermen and mermaids all lie upon the shore,
enraptured in this Isle of peace with beautiful decor.

I hear the tinkered elven song still calling from afar,
where quavered flutes ring wistfully to come to Zanzibar.....

William Rout

Sweet Rebellion

She is celestial -
the mother of the galaxy
with an expanding girth,
subtly dipping out of orbit
in a lunar revolution,
spilling bright epiphanies
in profound slivers of scintillation,
each beam an offspring
streaming from her soft brilliance
across the fringes of night,
molten by a deviating sun.

Her halo befits her like a crown,
the aura of her
lucent silhouette inspiring
constellations – as they borrow
a portion of her quintessential
light, the opalescence
perfectly mirrored in the
lux of each singular star.

Like mercury she quivers,
as her shimmering silver drops
disperse, painting twilight
with stardust confetti,
then having lulled the
universe to sleep,
she dreamily ascends,
settling into her
blanket of sky.

skkingrey

Silent portrait

The outline of your soft curves
Image in my eyes so welcome
So inviting to touch
Distraction so delightful

My emotion fill and
I need to be one with you
Need the lone time silence
The power of our vibrations
Converting our light to be seen
For timeless eeons

My hands quiver as I take up
My brush ever so light color
Forming in my imagination
I see our light your vibration
Your ora is my heart beat

Yet in this earth we co exist
You were created pure white
With a orange ora flaming around you

With canvas as my medium
I cast you into eternity
For all to see – admire
And display there envy
For they will never have known
You as I was blessed to share
This moment this intimate precious
time that we shared as one.

Drikus

The Death Of Xander Scott

His flame would not last long
once he retired from porn
to assist the poor
in third world countries.

We remember his heart
no anathema,
he was good and did die
young.

That crash tore off
part of his face,
he could never work
again.

The beauty of youth.
ejected so completely
he died incredibly old;
hopeless at the age
of thirty.

James C. Allen

The Waves of Time

As beauty flourishes and lilies bloom,
so will my love always be with you.
The rose may wither,
but the petal will never cry farewell.

The newfound years of spring
and the instructive years of winter,
how many we have spent together.
All were simple treasures.

The waves of time
and the laughter of youth
will forever remain, never hindered, never tarnished.
But one must continue to comprehend
and relish the enlightenment of life and knowledge;
life is both glass and gold.

Boardwalks are a symbol of the continuity
of life and learning.
To find a seal at the end,
is to be blessed with the guidance
of both angels and nature and the kiss of joy.
Animals bring life, for they are life.

Finally, upon old age rests a glorious nostalgia.

Abigail van Eden

Sharing Life With You

If I could write a love-song for a troubadour to sing,
I'd write about your love for me, I'd pen just everything.
I'd write about the milky-way, I'd write about our bliss,
I'd write about those gentle times, a smile, perhaps a kiss
to send me into raptures, to smile for ever-more
I'd write the words for Acker Bilk, his 'Strangers on the Shore.'

If I could write a love-song I would paint a sunny day,
with crystal waters, rolling hills and dreams that gently sway
that takes your breath and brings a tear when walking hand in hand,
in pastures green, in quiet glades or footprints in the sand:
But I would write remembering a fire, a rocking chair
the fear of loneliness, the tears, the thought that you're not there.

I'd write my love song through the eyes of this old ageing man.
I'd write about your caring smile that moulds the way I am.
I'd also pen a word or two about my peace of mind
and how your countenance reflects the love I seek to find;
but most of all I'd write about our perfect love, it's true,
I've found my heart, repose at last, while sharing life with you…

Dan Lake

Until then

I am not of those disingenuous ones
around here,
I dabble what I can with the words that spill
from my brain box,
I join them together to create a sentence and out comes
a type of poetry.
You read you like it, you leave a nice comment,
if you don't, you leave it,
but don't rant and bite behind my back
this I don't like.
just now I have run out of words,
so I leave my sentence incomplete
maybe you can complete it for me.
Until then............

Debra Joseph

The Sky Was Crying

THE SKY WAS CRYING,
as he abandoned teaching
with a thought to be much richer,
with a thought to to have a job, more decent,
than the one that he was doing recently.
what and where, that he didn't say,
he had just changed his honest way.
have, ex-colleague, a good day!

Ivan Petryshyn

Lavender blooms

Lavender blooms, come grace again,
of beauty in ethereal,
whispers swaying in the breeze,
my broken heart to heal,
no sunset on a harvest sky,
soothe my heart's dull ache,
a longing for my love's return,
this lilac bloom doth take,
it's scent upon the wing of prayer,
to my lover's heart,
awaken passion once again,
this bloom my love impart

Gassingon

One Ray of Hope haibun

In January, my husband expired with sailing clouds. I miss joie de
vivre that we tasted as one flesh. It is my opinion that together, as
one set of footprints, we touched this journey called life. It is
painful to pick up the pieces and live on, alone. With help from
above, a golden sunray will keep beaming. I have to till that one ray
of hope.
bamboo vases
wait on window sills
for May flowers

Colleen Selvon-Rampersad

My Autumn Garden

Now that my garden is asleep
There's not so much I must upkeep,
Although some leaves are hanging still
And each night brings a frosty chill.

The beauty of the summer's gone,
Only the rose will linger on
As flower beds no longer cheer,
So pinks and reds shall disappear.

The oriental poppy bows
As though these are her final vows,
I haven't seen a snail in weeks
A clustering in slimy cliques.

Last week the hostas bade, 'farewell',
Surrounded by discarded shell,
While snails have feasted at a pace
So intricate, like antique lace.

The peonies, with heads aloft
Now stand fatigued and brownly soft,
As breezes tremble trees so bare,
Like spinning windmills in the air.

And round my door great spiders creep
Mid silken webs they spy and peep,
But now it's cold they'll come indoors -
For Puss to torment with her claws.

And russets on the orchard floor,
A feast for badger's winter store,
Along with carrots and courgette
For when he ventures from his sett.

A nibbly mouse has locked his door
To sleep tight curled on leaves and straw

Yet squirrels still come down to see
The titbits I've put out for tea.

And sat upon a golden bough,
A blackbird tries to tell me how
His birdsong must now surely cease,
Unlike the chatter from the geese.

Now veils of rain will sweep the sky
And thunderstorms will surely cry
So I shall put away my spade
Until I hear spring's serenade.

Lulu Gee

The Sands

She lies beneath an oft pernicious sea
feigning, sleight of hand, a vulgar ruse.
Like a common cheat she'd often use
her guile to importune both you and me.

Beware, her shifting tentacles contrive
to jerrymander thought, invite you in.
Seducing, with an opportuning grin,
feigning homage might you just survive.

Countless sculls reside with sightless eyes;
deep within her bowels are sailor's hands
that wave to warn on-comers to the sands;
shrieking warnings through yon sea-gulls cries.

Fear not she whispers, am I not but grain.
Welcome to my soft and snug domain.

Dan Lake

The Trauma Of Being A Sensitive Boy

First it was Black Beauty, they split my soul
with that one.
Then during my most formative years, the jungle
of the hideous growing up, crippled by Mr. Sinclair.
I was those beasts slaughtered in the houses of demise
in Chicago.

I never put that one behind, instead it became my mantra,
my call to arms, the seeds of compassion sown a few
at a time.

And God, that horrible lowing, a train jumping track,
cattle car immolated by the burn
of diesel and disease.

Oh, Upton, why? If you had known me
the wolves might have been staid from my door,
but men are taught to hate, instructed in the finer points
of disavowing the importance of life.

Kill them all.
Those dumb beasts whose sole purpose,
we have determined, is to surrender
without even a prayer to spirit them home
before the mallet crushes their last thought
and they buckle to the ground.

I can't remove the stains from my mind.
I cry when I remember seeing the real thing
later in life.

All that blood,
all that blood.

James C. Allen

West Winds

Like lightning yearns for soil
drunken of moonlight
our atoms were magnetized
with a thunderstorm of sublime hope

That moment
my truths are a whisper
drowned in the depths of your eyes

I have marched against the west winds
where the earth is veined by dreams
The illusions still linger and dance with my heart
a graceful way of seducing the untamed

Which sky is your limit
when your thoughts are lost within the atmosphere
Oh it hurts to become
when a sore soul meets the burning sun

Let us jump universes
until the sea reflects
our stellar constellation
and the past is only a petal in a field of roses

You kiss Neptune's drops off my cheek
and my resistance dissolves
in a colourless sky

Bonnland, Jessica M

ENCORE! ENCORE! ~ *Sestina*

Elaborate extravaganza revues embrace players,
multifaceted talents or femme fatale flashed figure lines.
There's a mad dash to dressing rooms to change costumes
slap-stitched together for another romp across the stage.
A mish-mash of melody and melodrama lights
up theatre goers' minds, pulling chords opens curtains.

There's nothing threadbare about the opulent curtains
that raise, with a flourish, to reveal passionate players.
An opus of poetry and musicality delights
patrons responding with pathos to libretto lines.
A Diva delivers high C's that project volumes from the stage
while robust heroes emote with gusto in period costumes.

Character traits are captured with chic costumes
by seamstresses able to spin tales behind the curtains.
From quaint Camelot to brash Chicago the world's on stage
with song and dance scenarios performed by savvy players.
"Triple threat" action entices crowds back between red rope lines
after intermission bell gongs, strobe technicians dim the lights.

Lithe creatures put music to motions with solo highlights.
Elegant limbs undulate in barely there costumes.
Cakewalk, classic, or cha cha cha crosses culture lines.
A glimpse of Chorus Line shared auditioners' final curtains.
Jim dandy acrobats never cease to amaze as displayers
of highly orchestrated oneupmanship feats on stage.

Actors project sweeping smiles or scowled frowns as stage
whisperers Thalia and Melpomene compete for starring spotlights.
The script directs meaningful moods of consummate players
who adopt agonized or comedic postures in flimflam costumes.
Entranced in a Merlin spell, no fan rises until curtains
fall, when uproarious applause precedes frenzied exit lines.

The pit emits a sound symphony from scores of lines
conducted by Master Maestro who rules below stage.

String, brass, and timpani are concealed by curtains
while woodwind reeds are swapped under knees beneath footlights.
Some come dressed to the nines in formal costumes
and others wear gear in tune with carnival players.

The performance arts are curtain calls to collaborate lines
of communication between players who create a world onstage.
They slip, trip and grip the light fantastic in their crucible of
costumes.

By Laurie F. Grommett and Penelope Allen

As Monsoon Weeps -YaDu form

As monsoon weeps
in wild sweeps, his
heart leaps faster
to cast her woe
upon tomorrow's rainbow.

For brave Kyi Aung
freedom rang bells
she sang in hope
of wide scope, peace
will soon come when grudges cease.

Colleen Selvon-Rampersad

Lower Extremities

Long, smooth, and shapely
Her legs go on for days
My mind could wander upon her image
In oh so many ways.
Though I remove her from the confines,
Remove her from the page
By allowing her to walk off set
Yes, using those beautiful legs.
Wrapped in vegan leather
They shimmer in the night
Where they will do their duty
To hold this babe upright.

Maddie Vee

Rose Petals In His Hair

Oh, the man he was! I bade him kneel
and this he did, with glaring disregard
as though the floor itself were far too hard
to touch his sacred knees. With no appeal,
he set his jaw and waited for my speech.
His hand was cut. The petals in his hair
showed just the place he'd been, and we'd been there.
I knew that rose, in reds and milky peach.
But all the lies he didn't speak just then
were to my heart a poison and a blow;
no word disguised the reason that he'd go
and that he was not like my noblemen.
The grove's dark arms in which he'd gone to lie
held not a tryst, but meeting with a spy.

Streambed

I want to love

I want to love, but I'm not sure,
if I can trust you anymore.
Are you truly deviant and gone astray,
and felt the need to run away.

Would my heart break if I knew,
someone else was next to you.
So many questions I have to ask,
closure and understanding is my only task.

It hurts so much to be uncertain,
are there lies behind the curtain.
Do you have secrets I cannot forgive,
without the answers I can barely live.

All I wanted was the best for you,
but was your heart untrue, untrue.
But so far no answers I've received,
so I'm not sure what to believe.

My heart hurts in ways I cannot explain,
so much confusion so much pain.
But you have run so far from me,
so I'm uncertain how to be.

Starting over would be great,
but I'm not sure if it's too late.

Bob Cser

A Star Fell Down

Her love-letter reached me
unexpectedly
after walking
along a three days' path.

In the light of her love
I began to glitter
like a star
in the green sky!

Suddenly she wiped
my name
written in the coast
of her heart.

And I fell down burning
like a meteor
from the sky,
a handful of ashes
lying in the pyre
of delight and hope!

Sidhan Roy

A Retourne to Autumn

How sombre now are mornings with skies of pearl so cold,
as trees let fall their showers of reds and molten gold,
but over where my heart lies the harvest is complete,
he's looking to the sunset at fields of garnered wheat.

As trees let fall their showers of reds and molten gold,
beneath the wind now stirring lies something to behold,
before blue skies turn mournful above the quiet hills
and busy hands grow weary before the winter chills.

But over where my heart lies the harvest is complete,
where in fields of goldenness the earth smells apple-sweet,
yet when the day grows cooler beneath a lazy sky,
wood smoke curls reflectively where sheep and cattle lie.

He's looking to the sunset at fields of garnered wheat,
where blackbirds have departed with appetites replete,
while gazing at his acres of which he'll never tire,
oh, if only I were there to quell my own desire.

Lulu Gee

Little Beaver

'Cross the plains of Oklahoma
You will hear a folklore tale,
Of a brave called Little Beaver,
For his magic they'll regale.
You will hear his name in lodges,
On the prairies, hot and dry,
In the wigwams of the chieftains
Telling trappers passing by.

While the elders of the nation
Who no longer ride to wars,
Will narrate of Little Beaver
To papooses of young squaws.
You will hear he's a brave hunter
With a spirit in his veins,
From across loud rushing rivers,
To the dry sequestered plains.

Far beyond the plains the forests,
With jade pine trees growing tall,
They will talk about his exploits,
From the spring through to the fall.
They will speak of warring parties
And the visions he foresaw,
Of forthcoming wars of nations,
'Neath the flight of the condor.

He saw dangers in a crystal,
That he wore next to his heart
And with hissing from winged serpents,
Such dangers he could impart.
For two sunsets Little Beaver
Gazed into his crystal heart
To foresee a trail of tears,
Where the mountain ranges start.
So he called the tribes to council

And with wisdom spoke in peace,
Telling of the hissing serpents
With their wings of deep cerise.
From the Mississippi river
They would trek one thousand miles,
Little Beaver saw it clearly
When he saw the corpse stockpiles.

And some rode on mustang ponies
And some walked a darkened haze
Far beneath the eyes of eagles,
Where the bison freely graze
And the spirits looked upon them
As they smoked their pipes of peace,
As they smoked the pipes together,
Free of any war-paint grease.

And they marched with lack of water,
Overland and to the west
And they died in tens of thousands,
With their loved ones to their breast
And they said, farewell to rivers,
Where the fish were plentiful
And the land of their forefathers,
Where beauty was visible.

'Cross the plains of Oklahoma,
You will see the Cherokees
And you'll hear of Little Beaver
With his tragic prophesies.
You will also hear from Pawnee,
Kickapoos and Chickasaws,
Starved and beaten from their homelands
Exiled from their southern shores....

Lulu Gee

Reminiscence and . . . Readiness.

.... te igitur clementissimae Pater Noster...

No, no not vestments there look again.

Broad shouldered Eagle, not clergy,
wings folded, turned away, shield shaped in visual symmetry,
white feathered head--strong beak in profile,
perched, alone atop selected marker.

Master of all he surveys both right and left, to front and rear.

Straight in rank and file,
Stones and trees spaced and covered down.
Each Stone twin of fellows left and right—

("Left, Right, Left...")

uniform, silent.

("Parade... Rest.")

Set apart alone by single adornment,
individual names and dates.

Parade decorations, emblazoned,
proudly escutcheoned, earned, important, individual,

not pinned on at ceremony, neither grouped or patterned on display:
Cross, Cross, Star of David, Cross, Star, Star, Cross, Cross, Cross,
Cross, Cross...
Random marked, row on row fading forward into mist
beyond front ranked trees,
tall guidons,
coveted standards born heroically, held above the rest,
to mark Unit front rank and file, rally point of old.

And so platoons, nay battalions aligned

along manicured fairway close cropped, neatly groomed,
flat topped... like military haircut... once seen on youth,
here now at rest... at peace?

The Eagle, sitting priest like, centered on soldier grave marker
in posture-perfect readiness,
confident, relaxed,
still among the living, not tense, not slack.

The living at neither peace nor rest here,
No, here we have reminiscence and... Readiness.

Jack Mullen

For Those We Lost In The War

It hit her like a bomb,
"the other breast too?"
But then the indomitable
humor,
the flash of topiaried thought,
spruced from the ache
of stilbestrol cancer.

"At least I won't look lopsided
in a dress anymore."

The kaleidoscope chill
of pastel poisons
raced to destroy the
monster once again.

James C. Allen

Renew Year

The eagle is being set free,
in renewal he is born again
to fly as high as the stars, as fast as the wind blows,
to places never before seen
or to places he saw in the past but now sees with new eyes.

The year ends
A new year enters
With the promise of brand new days
We are given another chance to fly again
to make new beginnings or
to take new chances.

In a new year, we are set free,
in renewal we are born again
to fly as high as the stars, as fast as the wind blows,
to places never before seen
or to places we saw in the past but now sees with new eyes.

Francine Skye Morales Lentini

Biographies

of

Poets

Abhilaaj

I am a double postgraduate in Literature- English & Hindi also a Sc.graduate with a Dip. in Journalism. I write novels, articles/poems.

Some lyrics have been recorded at places like Sound cloud.

World affairs, sports, religion, films, cooking, drama and philosophy are my main interests.

Past life regression, Future life progression areas I am exploring keenly.
I am discovering the mysteries of life and am stunned at my ignorance.

Allen, James C.

Georgia, USA
Award-winning writer of modern poetry going back to the nineteen seventies. My first book "Saying Goodbye To Rue" published September 2014 by Shoestring Book Publishers is available from Amazon.com, Barnes and Noble, and Lulu.
I am a three-time winner of the prestigious Dr. Bruce Dawe O.A. prize, first for the poem, "The Final Viewing Of The Tulips" published by Prism Contemporary International Poetry Anthology, editor Ron Wiseman, 2015.
In addition, I was selected Prism Anthology Laureate, June 2015.

Recent Awards:
Winner: The Eye Of The Poet Competition for poem, "Across The Universe" December 2014
Printed in Prism Contemporary International Poetry Anthology. Editor Ron Wiseman, Australia.
Available from Lulu Independent Publishers.
Winner: Dr. Bruce Dawe Prize for poem, "The Pines, New York circa 1985." April 2016
Winner: W.H. Auden Prize for poem, "Diagnosis" April 2016
Both Appear in Prism Contemporary International Poetry Anthology. Editor Ron Wiseman, Australia and Jo Elle, Belgium. April 2016. Prism #19 Available from Lulu Independent Publishers.
Winner: Sylvia Plath Memorial Prize for "Winter Becomes Electra." June 2016
Winner: Clive James Prize for "Tennessee" June 2016
Winner: Dr. Bruce Dawe OA Prize for "Light Years Of An Exceptional Boy" June 2016
Prism #20 Available from Lulu Independent Publishers

Affiliations/Memberships
Life Member: Allpoetry
Fellow: Prism Group
Fellow: International Poetics Foundation

Co-Editor: International Poetry Fellowship Anthology, "Pepperoni Pizza" Sept. 2016.

Allen, Penelope

I've lived so many lives I have trouble figuring out exactly what I am. I know what I'm not. I'm no phony baloney doormat of a dame. I'm proud of what I've achieved which includes a roof over my head and a healthy pension. Blessed with a son who grew up and left home without hating me.
I'm friendly enough to welcome being called Pen if you're wondering. It's how I'm known in many circles and it's well within my comfort zone.

I spent many years helping workers on the shop floor and on a professional level because of my labour ideology.

Discovered poetry late in life but always was a writer of letters thanks to a mother who insisted upon things such as communication skills. It's been said that my vocabulary would choke a horse which I accept as a compliment. Since 2004 I've been able to declare I am a published poet! I'm a self taught poet who availed herself of lessons via the internet and am especially grateful to Conrad Geller who explains formats in language I can understand. I delight in exploring the idiosyncrasies of poetry styles and have taken a stab at many of them. I was an e-zine poetry editor twice on a volunteer basis and found it an enlightening and rewarding experience. Love travel, Dodge automobiles, history, architecture [especially bridges], art galleries, photography, museums, winters without snow, summers without scorching heat, living by the ocean and my Canadian Island paradise.

My condensed autobiography, in rhyming couplets, can be found here: Redneck Socialist
Collaborated on a 2013 Chinese Zodiac calendar by composing 12 poems to be featured beside beautiful Chinese cut-paper art.
Author of Zodiac Zoo
http://www.amazon.com/Zodiac-Zoo-Penelope-Allen/dp/1426946414
If you'd like me to mail you an autographed copy that can be arranged. Send me an IM if you are interested.
Poem: Bazaar Shades of Sorrow published in Dead Men [and Women] Walkinghttp://www.amazon.com/Women-Walking-Editor-Julie-Dawson/dp/1847289061
Poem: Aran Go Blah! published in KnitLit the Third
http://www.amazon.com/KnitLit-Third-Spin-More-Yarns/dp/1400097606
My first published work was Meeting Mike, a short story based on a real event on the Summer Solstice of 2003. The free PDF file can be accessed for download here:
http://www.thereisnocat.com/images/SOLSTICE.pdf

Arjuman , Firdous

Hi! I am from India. Poetry has been a passion that does not seem to cease since childhood. I have majored in English Literature and managed double gold medals. Besides online work, I have work published in paper. Well I have been on Allpoetry a while now and my indulgence in poems has simply increased. I have met some really wonderful people and read several excellent pieces. I am enjoying every bit of it.

Bissot, Joshua Joseph

it's our vocabulary that defines our ability to fathom that which the plaintive pedestrian mind will never consider - and in the moments where we challenge our understanding through our verbosity and comprehensive articulation, the wonderful gift of wisdom finds its way into our hearts Visit my homepage at poetrydig.com/

Blondell-Pitt, Deb

A student of poetry who lives in Canada.

Botello, Sandy Jo

Wife, mother, grandmother...live on a farm in the midwest... love music, sewing, gardening, homesteading, farm critters, life... photo circa 1981

Burson, Thomas

Thomas N. Burson Born in Key West, Fl. lived there for 7 mo. haven't back since. Quaker, went to Westtown High School and then Reed College, then George Mason and then ... Published in various anthologies, newsletters and the like. Love to perform at open mics and with jazz musicians. 65 now and still trying to grow up. Peace & Grace, Tom B.

Collier, Alf

I have a passion for writing poetry that began in January 2015, and it has not lessened since day one. I adore reading the souls of other poets from the words they write.

Crumbs.of.sorts

Andi
B.A.
University of Florida
English Speech Journalist
M.A.
University of N. Colorada
Administration & Supervison

maybe 'alone' is B.S.~
most over-rated.
maybe people are meant to be in sync with others: loving, laughing, crying, all of it. together. maybe people need people to feel honored and cherished.

I am all
and I am nothing.
it depends on the moon and the day.
I live with passion peppered with love and sometimes tears.
I am learning how to love all of me. I have been gifted a husband I cherish. we live with a four-legged child, who is named after my passion of NYC...BeCa....(Tri-BeCa.)

I am overly sensitive, emotional and dramatic. I am always near. I fill myself up by filling up others, sometimes I leave myself there.

Culliton, Cp

Patrick Culliton lives in Guilford, CT and has been writing poetry for a little over ten years. When he's not drinking craft beer or spending time with his adorable niece, he spends his afternoons working at D'Vine Bistro or exploring the New England countryside.

Cupsa, Ovidiu

Doctor of Philosophy, Maritime Transport Engineer Officer, University Professor, Writer and Poet.

Daws, Chris

To answer why my poems have form
and swing when I recite 'em
The human heart in iambs beats
so that's the way I write 'em

"Rhyme & Rhythm" a collection of my poems is available from Amazon.
There is also a kindle version. Just search for "Chris Daws".

I am happily divorced, by that I mean I am still friends with my ex. We have 5 grown up children and 2 granddaughters.

Donoghue, Susanne

I waited to be born until after all the A-bombs had dropped and have been seeking the peace of God ever since. My poetry records this beautiful journey. My husband and I now live in Ecuador nine months of the year and Chicago for three. You may find more of my work in Meditations for Single Moms (Herald Press, 1991) and Transcendent Joy (Amazon, 2015). Self-published Perfect Season in 1990. Someone invited me to All-Poetry a few years ago; I've found a happy home there. May all be blessed and healed. May all find their path to God.

Emery, Alison

A Wife, Nurse, Mainer, Author, Book Publisher, Poet, Novelist, painter, bunny mom, Aunt, amateur photographer, and all around care giver and artist.**www.shoestringbookpublishing.com**

Emery, Allan

Allan R. Emery is a Spiritual Counselor, philosopher, composer, poet, comedian, author and Reike practitioner who has published a co-written self help novel, co-written a young adult paranormal fiction novel, short stories such as Insights and Other Bothersome Things, Beerquest, Saucy Sonnets, Birdie Poop Poetry Book and an article on spiritual possession as a viable psychological diagnosis at the request of Dr. Jean Bruno Meric. He is the co-owner and chief executive editor of Shoestring Book Publishing. His music is available on CD: A Night With THE BEDSPINS.

He was fortunate enough to live in Farmington Maine, where a local professor shared his personal one-of-a-kind videotapes of lectures given by members of Wilhelm Reich's inner circle of psychoanalysts discussing his scientific approach to neurosis and psychosis. He also had the great fortune of knowing Kay Mora, a nationally known psychic used by over half-a-dozen police departments, who was famous for manifesting spirit voices that could be recorded on audiotape. Allan also knew Harvard's Psychology Professor David Perkins, who helped found a research program called Project Zero.

Allan has spent the better part of 40 years studying and comparing different scientific disciplines, logical-mathematical systems, psychological mechanisms and spiritual philosophies in addition to writing, and mentoring other writers and seekers of truth. He finds the methodology of organized academics to be prejudiced, limiting and counterproductive.

"Education in the US is run like a business, an assembly line mass-producing cookie-cutter graduates who can speak authoritatively on their respective subjects but are all but incapable of an original thought on any subject whatever, especially their supposed field of inquiry. It is completely counterintuitive and only by the resilience of the human spirit does our collective understanding actually

progress in spite of the attempts of higher-education to eliminate that potential."

Allan is one of those people who truly loves learning and yet no matter what he learns, manages to keep his mind completely open. He is your prototypical self-sufficient Mainer who belongs in the rugged country, far away from the rat race of city life. Allan R. Emery has healed a number of souls, but when I asked him if he would like me to mention how many souls he has healed he simply said he is- 'a humble satirist and all around irreverent spiritual guy.' So there ya' go, I think that pretty much sums him up.

Essama, Chiba

A poet at Allpoetry website. A member of the International Poetry fellowship -Anthology Publishing group. Had the honour to be published in their Alphabet Soup Poetry Anthology June 2016.
Poems published :
In Silence
Mystical Women (Rabi'a)
Human Grace
Come Fly With Me
Ivory Towers
Published again in Pepperoni Pizza Poetry Anthology September 2016.
I used to work at the BBC Overseas Arabic Service in London and had my own programme.
That's where I met my husband (Abed Al Kader Naguib) a TV director, script writer and a great man. We went back to the Middle East where I shared with him over forty Drama series for many TV stations in the Arab world.
I spent all my life on a quest for knowledge and wisdom. I did my best to be a good person, wife, mother, grandmother and I feel blessed.
I had my share of joy and sorrow but I guess it's all part of life's journey. I have no regrets, all is well.

Ezekiel, Ogbest
now a tyme to build a strong tower and bridge.
My page- www.ogbesteze.wordpress.com
my page- www.ogbestezekiel.blogspot.co.id

Gassingon
Writing from the heart..

www.writingfromtheheart.co.uk - Bespoke Verse & Speeches For All Occasions

Gee, Lulu

Lulu Gee lives on the south coast of England, she worked in corporate finance until her retirement and now writes full-time with her two dogs Teddy and Dolly never far from her side.

She is the author of two books of poetry written in collaboration with her husband the acclaimed poet Daniel Lake and who can ignore Miss Twizzy, the famous little mouse who went into print in 2013 and became an immediate success for Lulu through her love of fantasy and the natural world.

To date she has been published in over sixty anthologies worldwide and was delighted to be made an honorary director of The International Poetry Fellowship in 2013 and the same year won the Vera Rich memorial prize for her much acclaimed poem, 'Cumbria'.

Geiger, Paul

Korean war veteran. Retired biochemist. PhD Johns Hopkins University, 1962. I like reading, feeling the thoughts, hearing all kinds of poetry except long, long (especially maudlin) stories. Short pithy poems I love. Haiku I'm attempting, also other oriental forms. I particularly love the Intersection of Poetry with Mathematics ("Strange Attractors" by Glaz and Growney").

"Immature poets imitate,
mature poets steal."
--T.S. Eliot

Gilbert Eisenlord, Karen Lee

A semi-retired educator and therapist, I have loved writing poetry since I was a young child; it being mainly a hobby most of my life. It is only in recent years that I have been able to afford more time to focus on it. However I have been published several times in anthologies and won 'best poet of the year,' in 2005 and the 'spotlight' at allpoetry in 2008. I am also being published again in several anthologies, otherwise and through allpoetry; Prism and IPF. I usually don't brag about these things, but maybe I should more? I have self-published four books of my poems as well as an anthology for one of my groups that I run here.

Being pretty hard on myself, I am wanting to continually improve and try new things. I wrote free style with some rhyming most of my life but have gotten into more forms the past several years; particularly since joining allpoetry in 2007. I am now familiar with many forms, but I am forever wanting to improve what I know and try new ones. I just want to keep practicing my writing skills in varying venues. I like many poets -- Emily Dickenson, Plath, Shakespeare, Robert Frost and Basho, to name a few. I am as eclectic in my writing and choice of poets as I am spiritually. I also love art and photography, nature, animals, philosophy, comparative religions, astronomy and physics. I have two grown kids, ten cats and a dog. lol

There are two groups here on allpoetry that I run; A Group of Animal Lovers and People with Disabilities. I am an Occupational Therapy Practitioner who is strongly influenced by alternative practices in medicine. I also believe in and have applied the therapeutic and healing powers of the arts and writing to myself and others. In my spare time I have volunteered my time to human rights, environmental issues and animal welfare, which comes through in a lot of my writing. I am also a graphic and fine artist.

My other hobbies are photography and making music. I am also a teacher here at Allpoetry, of three classes; 'The Gentle Beginning Elements of Poetry Class', "Writer's Block', and 'The Basic Elements of Writing Poetry -- Intermediate Class.' Please feel free to check them out and join in! If you want the links, please message me. Thank you for stopping by to view my page. Below is an example of one of my recent poems.

The Cherry Blossom Tree Sprite
She first appears through early morning teal mists;
just before violaceous firmaments rise to sun's kiss.
Cheeks rubescent as the blushing cherry blossoms;
her figure emerges from trees' quintessential essence,
as aurulian warmth begins to surround her presence.

Long gilded hair, brushed flames of earths inner fire;
cherry blossom petals adorn her locks with desire.
Eyes still closed from night's nectarous dreams;
softly, sleepily; she exits from the trees,
as fair arms reach through the cool, silky breeze.

This beauteous cherry blossom tree sprite;
the gathering bees make way at her sight,
as she lovingly walks among her children of light,
she begins to dance and twirl in pure delight.
Down the walkway through awakening trees'
green leaves embrace, through meadows she weaves.

Radiant lips rival dewy florets' blooms;
eyes reflect blue skies; swirling clouds' plumes.
(The spiraling nebular translucence
of soft skin's opaline luminescence;
all of nature in spiritual transcendence.)
Pearls adorn delicately curved ears;
but what is that precious gem on her cheek, a tear?

Again it is time to sleep when golden sun sets,
as silhouetted trees retrieve what light is left.
She weeps as this glorious day must end,

for she must retreat from her family and friends.
Pensively, she returns down through vaporous path,
wishing that these precious moments could last.
Birds, bees and butterflies; all echo goodnight;
enchanted dreams, dear cherry blossom tree sprite!

Gilchrist, Ann

Ann spent her childhood on the banks of the Firth of Forth in Fife, Scotland. She came to Western Australia when she was 24. She won her first award for poetry in primary school and had been waiting for another ever since. She has, in her younger years, been a postal worker, check out chick, butcher shop assistant, nautical student, (still speaks rusty morse), police officer, painter, mosaic artist and gardener. She is currently a dental nurse. She loves to try and capture visual images of moments, memories and landscapes in poetry. She views her poems as canvases not requiring wall space. Creativity is an important part of her life, it helps to keep her relatively sane. She is married with five children and a young granddaughter.

Gogo, Carrie

Carrie Mercedes Gogo, a graduate of the University of hard knocks. Born in Historic Kingston, Ontario, Canada in 1975. She was unfortunately made to encounter loads of adversity in her younger days. She has been a Sexual and physical abuse survivor, an emancipated minor at age sixteen from Children's Aid Society. She never got the right atmosphere nor sufficient motivation for pursuing her education.

Carrie's writing styles are free verse and prose, Carrie is acquainting herself with new poetry forms, practiced in her spare time. Carrie's hobbies include reading, writing, photography and spending time with family.

Poetry for Carrie is a promise a commitment to stay current and genuine, with continuous encouragement from family and friends. Carrie is a member of the International Poetry Fellowship, currently, has three poems published "My Vow" and "Abyss" in Pepperoni Pizza Anthology, also has one poem published in Remembering Spring (A Poem Anthology) titled "Autumn's Arrival."

Carrie's strength of character is what propels her in Life, Carrie hopes to publish her book of poetry in the future, so stay tuned for that, "Wish her luck."

Carrie would like to thank IPF and those of you especially her most favorite poets/storytellers at All Poetry for your friendship and incentive towards achieving her pre-set goals and emerge a winner in her eventful life.

Green, Sue K

I am a wife, mother, grandmother, poet, photographer ... Both poetry and photography have opened my eyes to the world around me, have taught me to see things differently, make new observations, and given me a vehicle of expression that I never knew before. As a senior, and caregiver to my husband who is recovering from a stroke he suffered now over three years ago, 'precious moments' seem so all important to capture. I have never been one to overtly show my emotions; but as I travel my newest emotional roller coaster, I have learned that emotions are just a part of each of us, they need not be justified and it helps when I share. At first, poetry was just therapeutic for me. Now, I am reading and studying poetry as an art form. I have so much to learn and I find it truly a challenge. There is so much to be said about the world in which we live. Poetry affords us the vehicle with which to share an emotion, an opinion, or open a new line of reasoning. I believe it offers me some sense of control in an otherwise chaotic world.

Other of my works may be found at: http://www.skgimages.com and http://www.poetrysoup.com/me.SkG.

Published works available on Amazon.com and other retailers.

"From My Heart in Pictures and Poetry"
"Love Is Climbing the Rainbow"
"Storms of Stroke and Stroke of Pen"
"Exploring Paths of the Past"
"Rivers of Thought"

Grommett, Laurie F.

I've been writing on the Allpoetry site since October 21, 2013; my first pen was a lark, seven months prior (March 2013). I'm a self-employed teacher with my own business, which means I teach anything to anyone and believe that learning is for life! I'd always been a fan of poetry and decided to write my own after my 59th birthday; I finally had something to say. I adore my boyfriend E., my rescue terrier named Fig Newton, my friends and family (especially my son Gabriel). My poetry runs the gamut of genres. It's sometimes humorous, fantastical, or haunting, but always comes from within. Please come and chat anytime on Allpoetry.com. L.G.

I have just finished my 24th collaborative poem with Pen Allen of AP fame and am proud to share with you: (Poems can be found at Allpoetry.com)

1) ENCORE ENCORE ~ Sestina Collaboration
2) PURE-APPLE...WITH-CORE---Sestina-Collaboration
3) Bedazzled by Bling ~ Sestina -Collaboration
4) Pansys in the Flower Bed ~ Sestina-Collaboration
5) Shuffling Queens ~ sestina collaboration
6) Revolving Glass Windows ~ sestina collaboration
7) Fashion Falderal ~ Sestina Collaboration
8) Vassals of the Night ~ Sestina Collaboration
9) Buskers Act Bizarre ~ Sestina Collaboration
10) haiku (52 divided by 12)
11) Garden of Glass
12) Captured on Canvas ~ Sestina Collaboration
13) Strokes of Beauty
14) Hallowe'en HighJinks - Sestina Collaboration
15) Trumpet Time ~ Sestina Collaboration

16) Apheilon ~ Collaboration of Poems
17) Salisbury Stakes - sestina collaboration
18) Blithe Boy ~ Pantoum Collaboration
19) Of A Certain Age ~ Sestina Collaboration 20) Song of Swans ~ A Three-way Collaboration with JR too
21) Don Quixote, Man of La Mancha - Sestina Collaboration
22) Faye's Grand Fouetté ~ Mono-tetra with PenAllen
23) New & Out of the Blue ~ Sestina Collaboration
24) Pavlov's Butterfly ~ Sestina Collaboration

I've also enjoyed writing collaborations with my good friends Katie Hepburn, Sarah Allattt, Skye Darkholme and Scarlet Skies, members of the Eclectic Group here on AP. Both Sara Gosa and JR have given me the honor of writing three way pennings with Pen Allen as well. I have won gold, silver, and bronze awards with these poems. What an honor all these ladies bestow! Please check out my collaboration listings.

My poems have also been published in the Prism's Anthologies in May, August, October, November, December of 2014, and January, February, March, May, August, September, November, and December of 2015, February, April, June, August , October of 2016, January, February, March (also chosen for Sonnet prize), May (also chosen as May Poet Laureate), and July of 2017.

On May 7, 2015, I had my poem "Freedom's Will" featured on Page One of the Poets Collective.org website. Thanks for taking a peek. On May 19, 2016, I became a finalist winner in the 2016 Winter Park Paint Out Competition for my piece "Toasty with Orange Marmalade (A Tasty Sonnet)".

In June 2016, my poem "Accordion Crimes" was published in IPF's Alphabet Soup Anthology along with a few other brevity pieces as well. On December 8, 2016, my poem "Whispered Words" streamed on the nesbitandgibley.com poetry blog. Thanks much guys.

On April 22, 2017, I had my poem "The Matriarch of Spring" published in a fellow poet's (Monarch from India"s) anthology ~

SOUL OF SEASONS - A Bouquet of Poems - Spring Anthology 2017. I have eleven poems published herein IPF's Pepperoni Pizza Poetry Anthology.

L.G. Here's sundry stuff about me

My "Bio" in ABC

An apple a day Annie

Broadway baby

Chaser of the stars

Doubting "Thomas"

Ever searching for answers

Frog collector

Grace sayer

Home provider for rescued pup

Inspired by melodies

Jingle writer

Klee admirer

Listening, looking, learning

Mystery reader

Newbie

Overly sensitive

Pleasure seeker

"Queen For a Day"

Ruler of my realm

Sunflower picker

Taster of delectable delights"

Unashamed

Vehement about "clean"

Wonderer

Excited to be alive

Yearning

Zealous believer in making peace

Gupta, Arjita

I love to express through poems and like to play guitar.

♀ + ♂ = ♥
♀ + ♀ = ♥
♂ + ♂ = ♥
Love is love

When evening takes over life, it is not the end, but a bask in golden sunshine

Visit my homepage at blog.loanbaba.com/author/arjita/

My motto is: Go with the flow of your heart! express what you got to say

Gwynne Allen, Diane

Diane Gwynne Allen is from Michigan, U.S. She has a Masters in English Education from Florida State University. She been a member of Allpoetry since 2009, where she is the dean of education. A P is the place where she refined her poetry skills. She has helped edit several books with IPF, and has a few poems published in each of them. In her spare time she enjoys gardening and participating in the dog sport of, agility, with her four Border Collies and a Rat Terrier.

Hamby Goss, Melody

Words can either bring happiness and joy, or can create hate, and pain...use them wisely.

Harmon, Tom

I am 42 years old and live in the country , my life has been colorful and rough. I embrace my Irish , German , and Native American bloodlines. My poetry is my soul laid open for all to read. I write many styles and enjoy reading. Most of my earlier works were dark and fantasy as of late though I have taken a lighter side

Proud hillbilly and ridge runner , writer of swill and slop jar poetry lover of one woman , I call her Dixie Fire , she writes as well Loyal to a fault , I care not for those that prey on the weakness of others.

Hawley, RiAnne

I practice wonders, concretes, and detailed descriptions. I'm a poet, futurist, strategist, freedom lover, & ENTJ. I write haiku, tanka, dodoitsu, haibun, yaoi, & other Asian poetic forms. My story genre's include crime, spy, romance, nature, religion, and moonlight.

"if you want to be like the moon you got to glow like one" – me

Books I've Published:
https://www.createspace.com/6944952 - The Zen Palace (Tanka & Asian Poems) https://www.createspace.com/6932970 - Rosebud Pearls (Haiku) https://www.createspace.com/6833525 - Midnight Rosebush (Haiku)

Healy, Mary Lou

  Published novelist, columnist and poet, watercolor hobbyist, gardening and nature enthusiast...Occasionally surface in the real world and am always surprised by it.

My romantic suspense novel, "Gingerbread Man", is available on Amazon.com and others.
https://www.amazon.com/Gingerbread-Man-Mary-Lou-Healy/dp/1424139953 My fun look at such novels:
http://allpoetry.com/poem/6843495

Partial List of Publications:

Short Fiction: Girl Talk, Home Life, in children's publications; and in Amazon.com..short fiction program

Essays & poetry in: The Christian Science Monitor, Yankee Magazine, Mature Years, Maine Life, New Hampshire Profiles, ByLine, Upcountry, Grit, Harlequin Publications, & anthologies; and in Christmas-An Annual Treasury, by Augsberg Press; & Our Fathers Who Art In Heaven, anthology

Articles & features: Lewiston Evening Journal, Exclusively Yours, Milwaukee, Harlequin (Romance) Publications, The Vermont Weathervane, The Vermont Country Sampler,& other publications Shorts: Readers Digest

Humor columns: The Boston Globe, The Boston Herald, The Providence Sun Journal, Quincy Patriot Ledger, Healthways

Humor: Hallmark Cards, Rustcraft, Gibson Greetings, & others A few varied examples of my poems:

This Place http://allpoetry.com/poem/6786184
Rhyme And Time http://allpoetry.com/poem/6780913
Speculations On A Nebula http://allpoetry.com/poem/6673525
This Is How I Live http://allpoetry.com/poem/6864117
The Color Of Maybe http://allpoetry.com/poem/6861765
Rendering Darkness Null http://allpoetry.com/poem/6851119
Synthesis http://allpoetry.com/poem/6675963
Trompe L'oiel http://allpoetry.com/poem/6722181
Our Vines http://allpoetry.com/poem/6757229

Poems to Form:

Villanelle
Beauty Descending http://allpoetry.com/poem/6832160
Footsteps In Time http://allpoetry.com/poem/6789259

Terzanelle:
Susurrus http://allpoetry.com/poem/6800239
Like Minnows http://allpoetry.com/poem/6714134

Sestina
A Life Well Lived http://allpoetry.com/poem/6683225

Pantoum
Evening Sky http://allpoetry.com/poem/6776527

Sonnet Tiara
The Whole http://allpoetry.com/poem/6880641

Hollins, Stephen

I am loving writing poetry inspired recently by falling in love and walking the Camino Santiago de Compostela Spain.

 I live on Waiheke Island New Zealand. I specialise in Improv, Theatre, Story telling, Dance, Clown, Mime, Teaching and Building.

Hopkins, Barry
Visit my homepage at www.ivangalliver.com/

Horton, Thomas

Visit my homepage at www.facebook.com/thomashortonpoetry
When I'm not writing, I'm the marketing director for an international manufacturer My motto is: Dreams only come to us when we sleep. If we want something, and we are wide awake, we've got to go get it.

I've been writing poetry since I was five. It's a part of everything I am. I appreciate the craft of a well-wrought rhyme, but I usually write in free verse. Any topic can be poetic if the right words are applied.

Iff Ur Abs

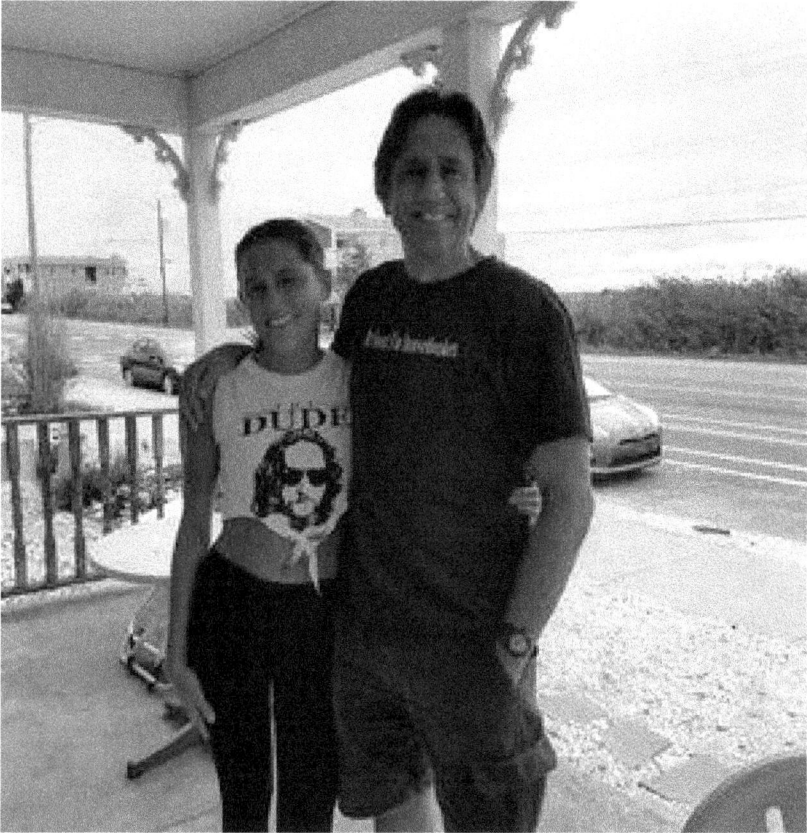

Once, a college athlete, now an athletic supporter, Iff has dropped the pipette, the beaker and the basketball for the pen and paper.

He hopes to write his tour de force someday before riding off into the sunset.

Ingram Melissa

I'm a 26 year old writer and photographer living life on the coast.

I love taking photos of the beautiful scenery and writing about moments from my past.

Izehi, Destiny

I'm here not to beat the best but, bit by bit, I pass my tests; be it good or bad, all ladders got steps, all fingers got their own heights; the reason for which life's a climb...

~poetry reflects the soul~ ~exposure influences literature~ ~poetry is what the eyes see; then what the mind thinks of it~

Visit my page: http://www.facebook.com/groups/destinyiizehi/

Jamesvm

James V. Martin

A man from Colorado, who's lived long enough to understand the sorrow of sorrows and appreciate hope and faith.

Johnson, Cody
allpoetry rank #455

"Buy the ticket, take the ride."

-my birthday buddy
Hunter S Thompson

But Hunter, what if the trail is free, shall I walk?

 "I don't care that they stole my idea. I don't care they don't have ideas of their own."
-Tesla

"Sometimes I make mistakes...sometimes I purposely choose the wrong way because it's fun and I like to live a little."
-me every time I do something stupid

Paper and pen poet
not copy and paste.

* I do my best eiditing
whlie drinking

Facebook page.. gotha tway.. almost 5000 followers check it out join the party :-)

my 3 favorites poems

Charles Bukowski
https://allpoetry.com/So-You-Want-To-Be-A-Writer

Mary Frye
https://allpoetry.com/Do-Not-Stand-At-My-Grave-And-Weep

Pablo Neruda
https://allpoetry.com/If-You-Forget-Me

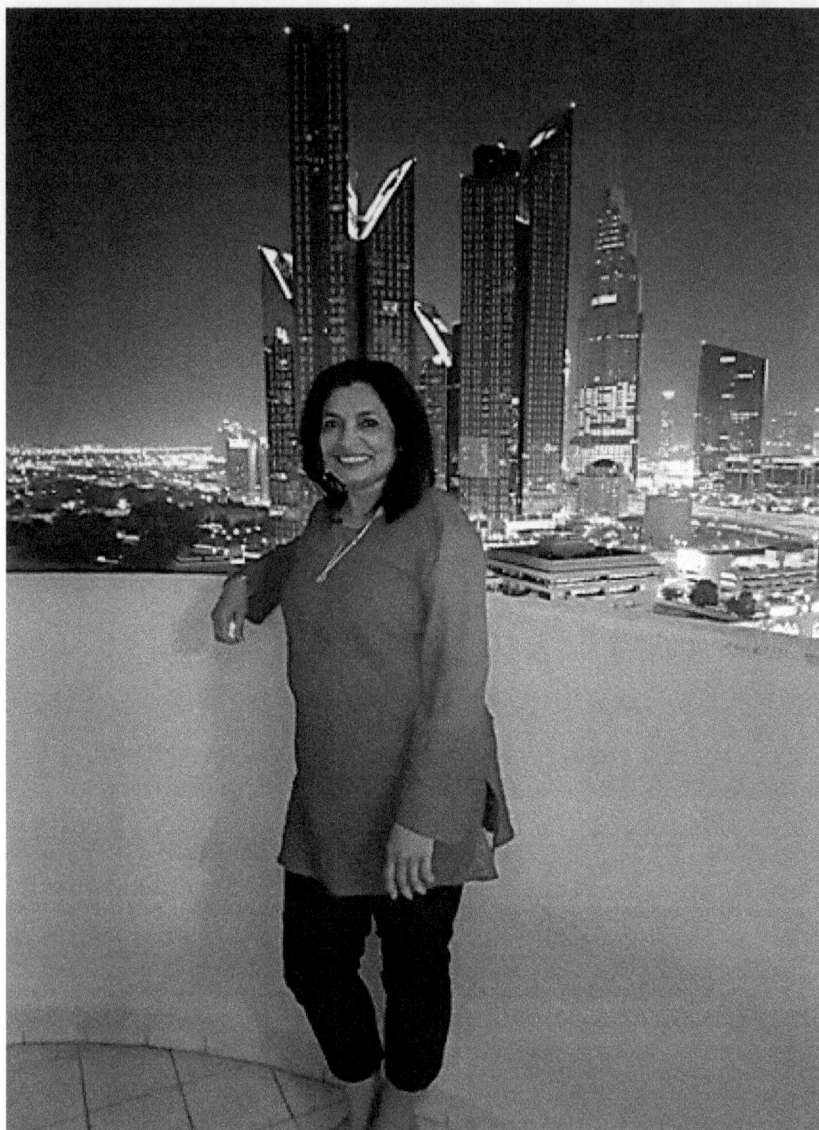

Joseph, Debra S.

I am a working widow and live with my three kids in Dubai in the
Middle East. Work as a PA tot eh legal department.

I have a passion for cooking, gardening and writing. I write
whatever comes from my heart and at the spur of the moment. I
have not been to any writing class, but manage to learn when I am
corrected. Writing comes to me naturally. I love to write!

I have my first book published and it called "Whispers from the Heart" & my second book is "Sail into the World of my poems" Both available on Amazon.

Karthik, Kiruthika

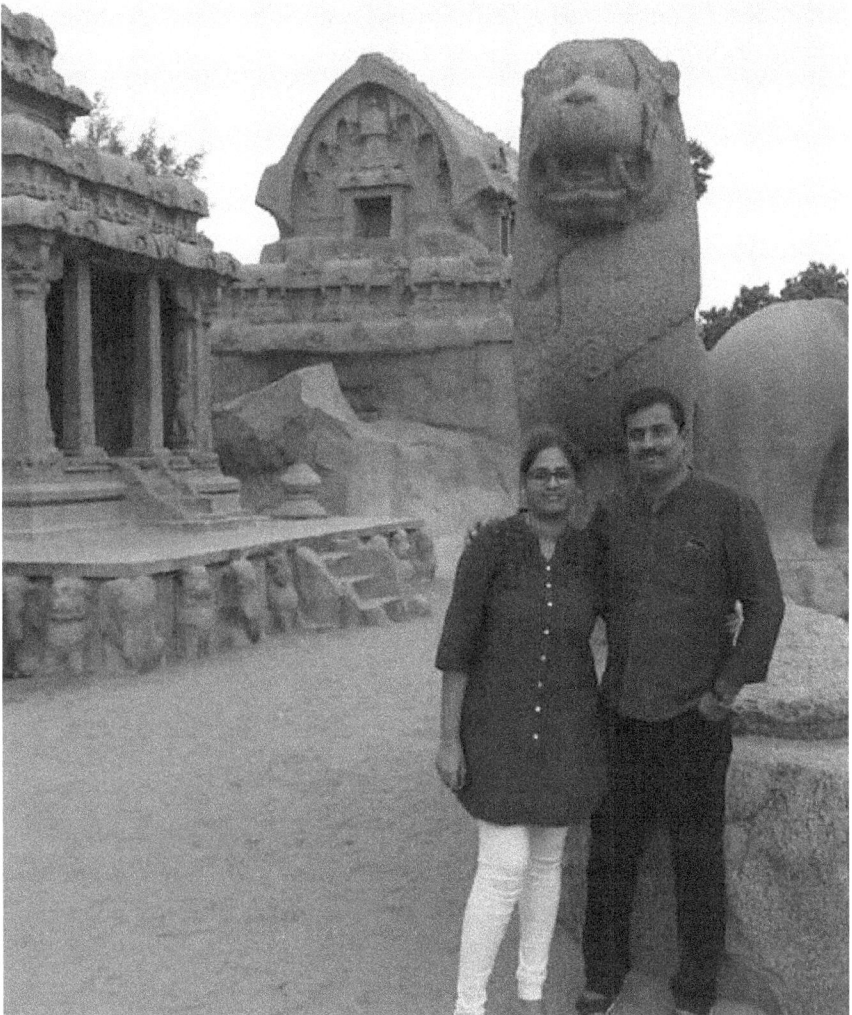

She was born in the southern part of India, Tamil Nadu ,Udumalaipettai. Completed her schooling in a prestigious school , Srinivasa Vidhyalaya Matric.Hr.Sec. school. After finishing her undergraduate studies in Vidyasagar College of Arts and Science, she went on to Karpagam University to complete her Masters. Her true passion, however, does not lie with computers as her studies would suggest. Her true love is in poetry.

To ask Sindhu to stop writing poems is the same as asking her to stop breathing. Her little brother was her first impression for writing poems. He was the first one who wrote a little, beautiful poem describing her as a "little princess ". She started penning her poems as Sindhu Selvi. AP is the place where she refined her poetry skills.

When looking at her poems individually, it would be hard to tell if they were written by the same person as their tone is always varied. They can bring tears to your eyes, make you gaze with wonderment at the world, or even smile with a deep sense of joy. Each poem she writes give her readers a glimpse into her colorful past and present, which is why no two poems of hers feels the same. Her poems are windows to her soul, and just like you can't judge a person with a single greeting, you cannot understand this poet with a single poem. Read all of her poems and maybe, just maybe, you'll get to know who she is.

She is married to the coolest person, she always says that. He never fails to read her poems and she knew he always does that with love and passion.

Her passion aside from writing includes gardening, dance, art, photography, sports and pets.

She dedicates her inking to her family,friends and a special person who belongs to a different world now, who brought her to this world, her sweetest and precious mom, Ms.Kalaiselvi Velusamy.

Thanks and Regards
Kiruthika karthik
(Sparkling river)

Kavanagh, Dave

I grew up in a tiny place in North Dublin. A fishing and farming village that boasted a population of three hundred souls when I touched down in 1964. It hasn't grown hugely since then. The people, characters and places of my not terribly happy childhood are the root of some of the writing.

I married Ber, my childhood sweetheart in 1986 and she has been good enough to stay with me since then. We have had 3 wonderful kids. Shaun was born in 1983 and we lost him in 1995 (The single worst day of our lives) Adam is 15 and Rou is 3. We are a loud, opinionated and mostly happy family. The kids are inspiration for some of my writing.

I can now be found at www.thebluenib.com. Magazine & Poetry Community

Keller, William Kenneth

Having what I feel a hard time expressing emotion through words, I tend to use story and mood to affect feeling. Hopefully I do this if not well at least enjoyably and with some degree of intelligence.

"Poetry is language at its most distilled and most powerful."
~Rita Dove

Keryn, Beth

Mountain girl, changing like nature. Loves poetry. I see my Wild Woman . Instagram: @bethkeryn

Kirkham, Brian F.

Born and Bred in Salford, Lancashire in the good old Northwest of England- Home of the Lowry Collection, Lark Hill Place and new home to the British Broadcasting Corporation and Coronation St (the TV soap). HND Graduate of Manchester Metropolitan Business school in IT. Sports Volunteer at Sportcity (Home of 2002 Commonwealth Games), I was also Team Leader for the London 2012 Ambassadors based in Manchester at Old Trafford and at Manchester University, where Brazil's Paralympic Squad trained. Currently Volunteering at Imperial War Museum North where I work as a member of the customer service team - been there since 2005 and love every minute when i'm there.

Lake, Daniel

The books that Lulu Gee and I Dan Lake have written "I Won't Sing if You Won't Dance" and "Our First Encore" plus my latest solo book with friends from around the world 'Electric Winds' are on release and can be purchased from the links below online, or from Waterstones or Amazon
http://www.authorhouse.com/bookstore/ItemDetail.aspx?bookid=6 3475

Further poetry of mine can be found on Jake the writer...see below.
http://www.jakethewriter.co.uk/Dan's%20Page.html

A poem that I'm proud to say Lulu Gee wrote for me a long time ago...

My Poet of Rhyme

He's all I ever want to read, my 'poet of the day,'
he gives me inspiration all the while.
His poems can be sensuous, heart-rending or risqué,
he seems to write a lot about a smile.
~

He pens rondels and sonnets with a flowing, perfect rhyme,
perfection oozes from his every pore.
He charms us with the seasons, especially springtime,
as we compel to read still furthermore.
~

He'll post to say my stress is wrong or my ti-tums are out,
but always he encourages my work.
We talk over our problems when our muses are in doubt,
with pens idle we know we'll go berserk.
~

He fills your head with pleasures in a tercet or quatrain,
or a tear, when he writes of something sad.
His forte seems to be in war and men who are in pain,
he wrote a heartfelt tribute to his dad?
~

His muse can take him anywhere he's 'Just a Simple Man,'
with poems from 'Safune' to 'The Snowflake.'
His rhyme is always perfect and his poems always scan,
Please let me introduce you to Dan Lake.
~~~~~

Lalli, Debra M

I earn my livelihood working with numbers, concrete tasks with definitive answers. I commune with nature, in reverence of all that is created, both seen and unseen. I play, gathering joy so I may spread happiness. I create as I continually strive to live a loving life. And when I write and draw, I always become all of these things at once An assessor, tax preparer, esthete, tai chi practioner, athlete, artist, writer, daughter, sister, aunt, wife, mother; a human being who continues to live life learning love.

Lindemann, Cliff

About Me ~ Cliff
Harlequined in many hats you will find,
A grandfather inside,
With a cap of a clown,
Of't wearing a frown.
Started as a teacher,
Then a trainee chef,
I still cook up a storm and a mess,
In my kitchen blessed.
Then found love in what I always wanted.
Horticulture and dirty hands,
Digging in the sands of life~
Growing trees to be there ~ far beyond my life.

In the garden of a swimming pool
I found my wife,
No ~ not a fool ~ I kept them all at bay and won the day.
Married had two kids.
Daughter born in Swakopmund in the Namib.
Where I landscaped Rossing's gardens in the desert.
Then a Son and from him 2 grandchildren,
The joy and terror of our lives.
40 years in horticulture retired ~ depressed ~ far tooo early.
I still dabble in new garden plants ~ my baby of this year ~
Capers plants growing in test tubes in a lab. The first ever born in
SA. The type you use on pizza and pasta.

Matin, Sept

Learned reading spontaneously at the age of three
Studied Persian Literature at high-school
Holding B.A, English translation
M.A student, English Literature

Thanks to Kevin for establishing such an amazing website,
Allpoetry, on which I could find a dear dear AP dad, the greatest
hero ever and the best flying fighter: Musedee , an amazing AP

grandpa, fabulously kind and caring: George (Dod) , and one sweet friend, a true angel Cinthia who are truly precious to me.

Love: bicycling , harmonica, walking at night, traveling, meeting new ones, books, comedies and animations, speed, height, scary movies, motorcycles, old and antique stuff, NON-luxurious house, cars, cellphones, etc., nature , pandas and orangutans, kites, jungles, ancient nations, music , Indians (native residents of America), climbing, and so many others!

I write short stories and poems. I work with a hip hop band as the lyricist, I teach ESL, translate books and stuff, write for local weeklies occasionally, work as an accountant.

Morales Lentini, Francine Skye

I am a retired Physical Education High School teacher and administrator originally from Brooklyn, New York. I moved to New Jersey after I retired. I often wrote poetry periodically from emotional reactions to things, but when I lost my significant other in the WTC attack on 9/11/01, poetry became almost a necessary outlet for me.

I am grandmother of two beautiful children, Gianna Marie 8 and Christian Jake, 4 and a half. I have three great nieces and nephews. I love children and loved teaching. I volunteer teach for my Church. I am religious and enjoy my faith very much. Many of my poems are faith based.

I write poems as they come to me. And they come to me all the time. Sometimes in the weirdest times and places, walking, shopping, driving, watching tv. They've been written on napkins, toilet tissue, receipts, envelopes or just about anything that could be written on. Sometimes I just write directly on the computer. Either way when the words want to come out they come out. I have never written a poem that I didn't complete in one sitting. It's like my pen just writes. I do enjoy writing and hearing what others think about what I write.

Mosley, Ben

Benjamin, Benny or Ben
 Long ago in the place of my birth I was given the name that I have. I am Benny or Ben to my family and friends, but I'm Benjamin, too, when it counts.

A few women have loved me in life, which is kind of amazing to me. I am not a great stud of a man, just respectful and slow with my hands. I was married until I was not, but two children were born for the world from the union I shared for a while. By their goodness the past is redeemed from the wrongs to regret, from the wrongs it is best to forgive and forget. I have loved and I've lost more than once but I'd love yet again, for a life when it's shared is just better, I think. I've regrets for whatever I've missed by not loving or trying enough. But regrets aren't the same as despair for the living that's still to be done.

I was not in the war of my youth though I served as a man under oath to defend with my life what was left of the law of the land of my birth. Through the times of my life I have played many roles. I've been seen as a sailor, a scholar, a teacher and preacher, a singer and poet, a boss and a worker, occasional lover and often a lout. I may wish I'd been better in roles I have played, but I'm fully aware I might well have been worse.

I've been under the sea, and I've walked on the shores of a lake in the sky. I have seen the horizons of plains which extend to the distance of sight. I've watched as the sun rose from the sea, and I've lain on a beach as it set. I've debated with elk in the woods and with snakes I have met on my treks. I have lived in some houses of brick and a camp by a creek in the trees. I have written some words in my life, and I've drawn a few pictures of things. I have sung for a drink and a kiss. I've been knocked to the floor now and then. All the singing and kisses I loved, and the floor never held me for long.

There are things I have studied in school and conclusions I've come to myself. No religion compels my belief in the God who exists over all. Call it faith in a something unseen or conviction from all that I see, for whatever has been or may come, in design more than chance I believe.

I am older than young, but I cherish the hope of becoming still more than I've been. If the times of my life here below should continue for years or a day, I'm expecting the world to go on as if nothing had happened to me. But whatever befalls, in the fullness of time I shall go to my God in the grace that he gives to continue my life in the age without end. It's from all that has been I have come and to all that's to be that I go. In between is the person I am, whether Benjamin, Benny or Ben.

A note about trophies displayed: As a user of the Classic AP site, I can remove trophies displayed on my profile page. Like most long-term members of AP, I have been awarded hundreds of trophies by various contest hosts. But showing all those trophies began to seem like keeping score relative to other members of AP when I should just try to be a better poet than I have been. I choose to display only the trophy most recently won, and that simply because it makes it easier to review trophy-winning poems when having won a trophy is a qualification for entry in another AP member's contest. I doubt that many of us consider trophies won to be a measure of ourselves as poets, but some undoubtedly do. For the counters or discounters of trophies, may you continue to improve as poets for yourselves and in the estimation of your peers.

Morka, Emilija

Emilija immigrated to the United States in 2002 at the tender age of 6 from her home country of Lithuania. She lives in the Chicagoland suburbs. Within the past year she has dropped out of college, become a pothead, ditched the pot, gotten her license suspended, gotten a haircut, gotten a full time job at a daycare, and has decided to emigrate. Nice job, Emilija. Favorite authors: Edgar A. Poe

Muir Alistair

Born 12/05/60 in Scarborough, Yorkshire, England. I have just had my first book published, "Cold Turkey" of which I'm very proud.

Mukherjee, Rajkumar

Rajkumar did his post-graduation in commerce from University of Calcutta. After retiring as a banker, he went back to his first childhood love, poetry. His poems were published in School and College magazines, local journals and even overseas journals e.g., Prism at regular intervals. During his college and university days, he edited and published number of literary journals from Calcutta and Purnea, India.

His first book of poems was published from Calcutta in 1975. In 1980, he edited an anthology of poems on Tagore with contributions of eminent poets of Bengal and Bangladesh. In 2009, two of his books were published from Calcutta. One was a translation of Maurice Carame book , ''Songs of Beginning' from French to Bengali.

One of his latest books, 'Soul Searching' was published in September of 2016. He is a regular contributor to www.poemhunter.com, www.mypoetryforum.com and www.allpoetry.com.

His poems are regularly published in Prism international magazines, IPF anthologies viz A.S.P.A, & P.P.P.A. and Ink Angels & Open Your Eyes printed anthologies of the allpoetry.com.

Mullen, Jack

Younger than Spring time, older than dirt.

Nazeer, Dr. Asghar

I am a medical doctor with an MBBS, MPH, MHS and DrPH from Johns Hopkins USA. I started writing poetry recently. I only write end-rhyming couplets. My intention is to convey my ideas, thoughts, and emotions on common subjects of everyday life in plain language to wider audience, whom I wish to feel that I wrote what they have always desired to say. To know more about me and to connect on social networks, please visit the links:

Dr. Asghar Nazeer – A recent JIDC author!

http://blog.jidc.org/2012/04/12/dr-asghar-nazeer-a-recent-jidc-author/ --- Google+ URL google.com/+AsgharNazeer ---

Twitter: asgharnazeer ---Dr. Asghar Nazeer

LinkedIn: http://sa.linkedin.com/in/drasgharnazeerlinkedinprofile

Dr. Asghar Nazeer Facebook Personal Page:

https://www.facebook.com/AsgharNazeer?ref=tn_tnmn

Dr. Asghar Nazeer Facebook Community Page Viewable by Public: https://www.facebook.com/PicsAndPoets?ref=hl

Delta Omega Honorary Society in Public Heath Mentor Network - Mentor Detail Mentor Dr. Asghar Nazeer

http://www.deltaomega.org/mentordetail.cfm?id=63

Delta Omega Honorary Society in Public Heath - Member Spotlight
Dr. Asghar Nazeer, MBBS, MPH, MHS, DrPH Delta Omega
Member (Alpha Chapter)
http://www.deltaomega.org/memberSpotlight/Nazeer.cfm
Dr. Asghar Nazeer, Alumni Notes, Johns Hopkins Bloomberg
School of PublicHealth http://dev13.jhsph.nts.jhu.edu/alumni/class-
notes/classnotes/grouped/2000/DrPH
Lifetime Members Delta Omega Alpha Chapter, Johns Hopkins
Bloomberg School of Public Health:
http://www.jhsph.edu/alumni/alumni-associations/delta-
omega/membership/lifetime-members.html
Global Journal of Medicine and Public Health Editorial Board
Member http://www.gjmedph.org/editorialboard.aspx

Paavolainen, V.S.

38 years old father of two born in Helsinki, Finland, but lived most of my life in middle Finland town of Jyväskylä. I worked over ten years at Post of Finland as a newspaper deliveryman, planner and head of newspaper delivery. I have studied in University of Jyväskylä majoring in world history in my youth and business in university of applied sciences in Jyväskylä recently.

Poems I have written since I was 14 but never in the same intensity as recent couple of years. Writing has always been a vent for me to let out pain. Mostly I write dark writes of pain but I try to be more versatile these days. Since I got active with writing it seems that writing got active in me and many time I am compelled to write; I never leave anywhere without pen and paper. These days I write both in English and in Finnish and then translate the text to other language which I consider a good exercise.

I am the odd fish in the tank that hardly ever gets understood; no matter what the language is. People have hard time following my thoughts. Same goes for my poems in general though some are quite simple too. I do write blogs in Finnish and English on poetry. And in Finnish some other blog. My English poem blog you can find here: http://poemsonmistyhazebridge.blogspot.fi/

Pappas, Chrysanthy

Chrysanthy Pappas, a poetess of Greek decent. She moved to the United States from Rhodes, a little Greek island, located in the Aegean Sea, when she was only three. She is an eclectic woman with a myriad of passions. Among them are photography, painting, playing her piano and dancing. But most of all she enjoys singing. She began her poetry career with an award winning poem at the very young age of six, being particularly proud of a certain poem because she wrote it in English, her second language. She resides in Sedona AZ where she recently relocated from Sarasota Florida, here she continues on through her journey in life and in poetry. She is an big animal lover and her romanticism is wonderfully infectious as it comes through, in the joy of her poetry.

Petryshyn, Ivan

Ukrainian-American. Studied in Europe. some courses of interest-in the USA. Independent Researcher (Linguistics), Educator,

Interpreter and Translator. Knows fluently English, Italian, Polish, Russian, Ukrainian. Some other languages- non-fluently. A member of the ISPS and the AAP (at present).

Pier, Kaleb

I am a rock.
I am an island.
I am the walrus.

The following are my favorite poems of my own. They are in no order, except the top entry which I consider to be my finest work, which can be found at my Allpoetry.com homepage, Iambthewalrus:
Denim Kills
Zero Six Zero Seven
At the Bottom of the Hill
Neon Halo
Fisher in the Quake
De Bom Humor
Ocean Swell
Connections

Tiger Moth
'Til Tonight
Where Something Was
The Proof
St Dismas Church, Maryhill
Walkerville

My motto is: The poets are just kids who didn't make it and never had it at all.

Rangorth, Satheesan

Hi I am from Kerala a state situated in the south western tip of the subcontinent. Poetry is my passion. I think i am not a poet. I am just a man standing on the shore of poetry with respect and awe. The most beautiful poem ever created is nothing but the nature. I believe that. I scribble some words in the format of poem and i do not know if it becomes a poem. Ah my full name is Satheesan Rangorth. Dear friends I am pleased to announce that I have published a collection of my poems in a book titled as SNAPSHOTS OF A FIREFLY. The book is available on line at AMAZON.COM OR AMAZONGLOBAL AND FOR Indians it is available at AUTHORSPRESS.COM

Rao, Shobha S.

An eternal student, I love learning just for the sake of learning. So I first studied to become a veterinarian and then earned my Ph.D. in physiology and pharmacology, I worked as a drug discovery scientist. I then did my exec-MBA. I now have made a mid life career transition. I have now started my own personal and executive coaching business. http://acoachingcatalyst.weebly.com/

Reed IV, William J.

I'm a Sci-Fi & Horror Novelist, A hopeless romantic, A song writer mainly in the style of the Blues I have played the Blues Harmonica for the past forty-three years. I started writing poetry at the age of eight. That was fifty years ago. At the age of eleven, back in 1969 I had completed a small 40 page booklet of poetry. Which was published when I was thirteen, way back in 1971, when I decided to become a Hippie Peace, Pot & Micro-dot, Dude, Well not any more Hehehe

I have recently finished the final edit of my very first full length 385 page Science Fiction Novel called... "The Guardians" I have decided not to do a vanity publishing on Amazon.com.

Instead I am following a strict set of guidelines to enter into a contract with an Agent. Who will market my book to all the Major Publishing Houses. I write poetry for the love of writing poetry Novels I write... For the money! Heheh

Roy, Sidhan

I am how I am... A poet lives in quality, not in quantity... Simplicity is the soul of a poem...Baramesya(Puncha), Purulia, West Bengal, India

Saha, Sandip

Sandip is a chemical engineer and doctorate (PhD) in metallurgical engineering by profession. He has retired from service and of 64 years age. He has got three awards for his scientific work and 33 publications on his scientific research work including three patents. His research work can be seen in the web page:
(https://www.researchgate.net/profile/S_Saha4).
His hobby and passion is writing poetry. He has published two anthologies one of which, Quest for freedom, is available in

amazon.com(https://www.amazon.com/Quest-freedom-Dr-Sandip-Saha/dp/8182532299/ref=sr_1_1?ie=UTF8&qid=1454597369&sr=8-1&keywords=Quest+for+freedom+by+Dr.+Sandip+Saha).

He is a life member of The Poet r y Society (India).

His magazine publications:

1. 'The city of Mumbai' in 2016 Poet's Showcase and Yearbook by
   Poetry Press Publishing International,
   Toronto, Canada, (Print)
2. 'Terrorism can be defeated' by Society of Classical Poets, New
York on
   9/9/2016 , USA (Web)
3. 'It is India' by Taj Mahal Review VOL. 15 NUMBER 2,
   Dec., 2016, India (Print)
4. 'Flood in our village' by Oddball Magazine, Somerville,
   Massachusetts, USA, 1/11/2017(Web)
5. 'Before journey is finish' by Snapdragon, (Web)
6. 'Ecstasy' by felan poetry and visual art, issue 11, page-29, May
2017,
   (Print)
7. 'Virgin mother' by Oddball Magazine, Somerville,
   Massachusetts, USA, on July 11, 2017 (Web).
8. 'Tune of nature' Published in June 2017 Vol. II No. VI issue
(International
   page) of Better Than Starbucks Poetry Magazine, Florida, USA
(Web).
9. 'He is mine' Published in June 2017 Vol. II No. VI issue
(International page)
   of Better Than Starbucks Poetry Magazine, Florida, USA (Web).

Senghor Kasi

My book, "Is Like This" can be found at Amazon.com and Xlibris

Singh, Madhu

Please check out books with some of my poems:
Inedible indelibles Volume 1, and Remembering Spring

Skidmore, Don

A collection of reading rooms,
a library of places and times,
a place for you to haunt,
nibbling on my rhymes.

Stay a while. We'll have tea.
Choose a list to turn a key.
https://allpoetry.com/list/by/Room%20Keys

skkingrey

I'm totally in love with my 10 grandchildren. Poetry is my escape.
I doubt anything I say will shift the earth on its axis.I have learned
more than I thought possible from my associations on AP. I feel
like I've taken a creative writing course for the last four years. I
have wonderful mentors who have guided meto becoming a better
poet with a greater vocabulary! When I'm not writing, I'm dreaming
in black and white My motto is: I bought a Mickey Mouse watch
so that I don't take myself too seriously.

Slotnick, Joe

poetry is a powerful force to fend off the estrangement and apathy
that block our mindfulness and natural joyfulness. And
interconnection to others and nature. I grew up in bucolic Lancaster
county. (i am not Amish by the way.) I now reside in Philadelphia
Pa.

My theory on composing poetry:reading and analyzing a lot poetry
seems to facilitate or sensitize one to elements of the writing good
poems,facilitates and sharpens the process of composition;words
saturate meaning.poetry, I feel, falls within the realm of music and
different laws apply. However, rules of grammar still apply to a
certain extent.I play piano and thus,I am partial to alliteration and
assonance, rhythm, meter, line length, and flow factor.. the musical
aspects of poetry. I believe all great poems have these elements. I
enjoy meeting other on line poets AP. poets are a rare and
unappreciated species, a dying breed? we poets are sensitive souls
and need to stick together, Let's stick together and keep poetry
alive! It's not just a passing hobby. It's our passion.

I hold a BA in English from The PA State University.

Szankowski, Robert

Robert Szankowski was born in 1979 in Union, New Jersey. He now resides in Hilton Head Island, South Carolina. Robert has a modern style of poetry influenced by many before him, from the sonnets of Shakespeare and surrealism of Arthur Rimbaud, to the love poems of Pablo Neruda and the imagism of William Carlos Williams. His books available for sale at Amazon.com: "Five Years: New and Selected Poetry", Swimming Lessons" and, "Fishbowl Pornography".

Terry, Mark Andrew James

Mark Andrew James Terry is still working as a brand and messaging specialist in Orlando, Florida, where he lives with his wife of over thirty-six years, his son (still in college), his cat Miss Kitty (Gun Smoke -era) and a raccoon who does not claim to be part of the family. His daughter lives nearby. Also chiming in are about a gazillion frogs who serenade from the trees and lush lake-side landscape of his home in Orlando, Florida. He is published in over a dozen anthologies and has been honored with the appointment as Director Emeritus of the International Poetry Fellowship. In his role as Trustee Emeritus of the Albin Polasek Museum and Sculpture Gardens, he founded and manages the Winter Park Paint Out International Poetry Competition, illuminating the poetry in art and the art in poetry.

van Eden, Abigail

I've always had a sincere passion for writing. Through the power of written words, I can freely express my thoughts, philosophies, and myself. As a child I would write short stories, whatever came to mind. Enchanted, beautiful landscapes often would entail.

Since a young age I have thoroughly enjoyed the literature of J.R.R. Tolkien, C.S. Lewis, Ralph Waldo Emerson, Mark Twain, and quite a many wonderful more. Emerson's "Nature" essay has very much inspired me. My poetic "flow", or style, is of my own uniqueness, however, I have learned much literary intelligence through such incredibly exceptional and brilliant writers. I grow more fond of poetry day by day, and my gratitude toward these men is of great abundance. 18th Century Europe is a time in history I simply adore learning about. Baroque and Rococo art are lost beauties; glorious interpretations of God's magnificence, splendor, and awe. I long for a resurrection of such art. Van Gogh's marvelous artwork fascinates my artist eye. In heaven, someday, I will wish to converse with the virtuosic Post-Impressionist. I also enjoy classical music; Handel, Bach, Chopin, Liszt, Ravel, Satie, and so many others are just a few of my favorites.

Life is interesting for me; I often feel inhibited, misunderstood, and rejected. Perhaps, it is an unfortunate part of my INFP personality. I "over-analyze" just about everything. For those who know me personally, hand sanitizer is a constant passenger in my pocket. I have perfectionist qualities that inhibit my everyday activities. I am a bright and comical person at the party. But in reality I have many introverted sides. I don't seem to ask many questions about a person when engaging in a conversation with them. I actually tend to get quite nervous and incredibly anxious at times when around others. It is a hard thing for even myself to understand.

All that is gold does not glitter,
Not all those who wander are lost;
The old that is strong does not wither,
Deep roots are not reached by the frost.

From the ashes a fire shall be woken,
A light from the shadows shall spring;
Renewed shall be blade that was broken,
The crownless again shall be king."
— J.R.R. Tolkien, The Fellowship of the Ring
~ ~ ~ ~ ~ ~ ~ ~ ~ ~ ~ ~ ~ ~ ~
"I'm just a human with a pen, and an imagination of some sort. Simply put."
- Abigail van Eden

Mr. J.R.R. Tolkien, a true inspiration of mine.

"No picture of life can have any veracity that does not admit the odious facts."
- Ralph Waldo Emerson

Wakefield, Madison

My horses are my life. The rest is just details.

Wass, Michele

I've been writing since I was 11, which is a very long time. It just came to me. Mother had a poetic bend, too, though, so I guess it came to me naturally.   Took writing classes in high school and college, but in the last 8 years have done more writing and more improving than ever before. Published in College newspapers, some newsletters and four IPF anthologies. Love gardening, blues, mysteries and cats. Oh, and my husband of 43 years.

When I'm not writing, I'm planting flowers, listening to the blues or playing with the cats and thinking of things to write.

White, Dennis L
Dennis is the father of Triplets & Twins. He has been writing for 16 years, he enjoys experimenting with different forms of poetic expression. He hails from Carleton Michigan, a town named after the famous Michigan poet Will Carleton. He leads a writers group in Wyandotte, Michigan. He is a member of the Poetry Society of Michigan and also the National Federation of State Poetry Societies.   His poetry may be found in a number of poetry anthologies and he plans to release a few poetry books of his own work when he retires from Ford Motor Company next year.

Wiseman, Ron

JUDGING A POEM! [I've used this system or something very much like it for half a century from great poets in an academic situation to judging regional contests and even an Australia wide contest.]

Consider Aptness of title last!

Form/Style — the character of the poem, like Rhymed and Metered (RM) or Free Verse (FV). Each poem was looked at for what it was and not compared to others.

Rhyme/Rhythm — whether rhyme and/or rhythm were a characteristic of the poem, and if so, whether the rhymes were natural and sensible or artificial and forced, and whether the rhythm (which also applies to free verse) was consistent with the character of the poem.

Poetic Devices — the number and effectiveness of those poetic elements that raise poetry beyond prose — there are at least 15 of them, including rhyme, alliteration, personification, and so on. Without their use, the writing becomes prosaically prose.

Comprehension/Coherence — do the ideas presented hang together to create a whole? Is there "meaning" to the writing, and is that meaning realized?

Mood/Imagery — does the poem illustrate its message — can I feel the feelings and/or visualize the images presented? How significant are those images to the purpose of the poem?

Word Selection(diction) — has the writer chosen the words of the poem to enable the poem to reach its intent? Are there clichés or overused imagery (we know the sky is blue) to weaken the conveyance of meaning?

Scope/Significance — does the poem deal with the human experience, and if so, to what extent is the poem successful in adding to our understanding?

Line Endings/Line Breaks — are these visual aids used successfully to create emphasis and to carry the reader to the main significance of the writing? In free verse, are the line endings used to create emphasis, and are the line breaks used to create a longer pause that is significant? Read aloud, the poem should sound well.

Punctuation/Spelling/Grammar — does the poet respect our language conventions and provide punctuation to aid the reader in understanding of the poem? Do spelling errors interrupt the flow of the poem's language? Are there distortions of word order that seem artificial and obscure meaning? I do understand the e e cummings effect and respect it.

Content Realized — the poem had a purpose when it started out — did the poem realize its intentions? Does it lead naturally to its conclusion?

Universality — is the subject matter of the poem meaningful only to the poet, or does it apply to the human condition? If it were translated into another language — German, French, Spanish, Italian, Afrikaans, etc. — would it still be meaningful to a reader in that language?

Total: the accumulation of points in the ten categories. A poem earning 85 points or greater went into a pile for secondary consideration. Poems earning fewer than 85 points in this accumulative system were dismissed from further consideration.

I read every winning poem at least three times. In my first reading, I aimed to understand the poem—where it started and where it ended. In my second reading, I scored the poem on my Evaluation Sheet, analyzing the elements involved as fairly as possible. When all scoring of any month's submissions had been completed, I re-read the poems selected for further consideration and selected those that "moved" me emotionally and/ or intellectually in appreciation of the message.

This technique of evaluating poetry served me well during the years I acted as Poetry Editor. Now I am frequently asked to judge poetry contests, and I use this system of evaluation to enable me to do more than merely react to words.

And in my own writing, I find this system of evaluation helpful to see whether I have captured the poesy or poetics needed to convey the feelings I'm concerned with—does what I have written really capture what I was aiming for? If my score in any column is low, I know I have to improve that element in the poem. The ruthless objectivity that the form provides helps to focus the revision process on what needs to be done. That minimizes what we often encounter as dissatisfaction with our work, without knowing why we are not satisfied.

If our aim in poetry is to condense emotion to its essence and capture the human condition in legible form, anything that helps us to do that well is a useful tool. I hope my experience and use of this evaluation system will benefit others in judging their own work and finding what needs improvement or revision, without the agony of having strangers rip into the work or ignoring its purpose or using mechanical means with a great faith in numbers such as autoranking.

Visit my homepage at www.pentepoets.com/ron-wiseman.html
When I'm not writing, I'm a writer of poetry & creative writing teacher during retirement; University Third Age at present.
My motto is: I seek to have poets published so they can behold their better poems together with that of others in fine anthologies. I founded Winklings; On Viewless Wings; Prism. I do write poetry.

Wright, Bethany S.

I am a Christian; this is the center of my life. I am married, with six children and fourteen grandchildren: we have 10 grandsons and 4 granddaughters.

We all attend the same church, and what a blessing it is to look about me on the Lord's day at all those beautiful faces turning to smile at me as we worship together. What wealth or fame could measure up to that? I am most blessed. The passion of our lives is so fittingly related in the words of this hymn, written by 16-year-old William R Featherston:

MY JESUS, I LOVE THEE

My Jesus, I love Thee; I know Thou art mine.
For Thee, all the follies of sin I resign.
My gracious Redeemer, my Savior art Thou;
If ever I loved Thee, my Jesus, 'tis now.

I love Thee because Thou hast first loved me,
And purchased my pardon on Calvary's tree.
I love Thee for wearing the thorns on Thy brow;
If ever I loved Thee, my Jesus, 'tis now.,

I love Thee in life, I will love Thee in death.

And praise Thee as long as Thou lendest me breath.
I'll say when the death dew lies cold on my brow,
If ever I loved Thee, my Jesus, 'tis now.

In mansions of glory, and endless delight

Wright, Bobby Jean

Four things to learn in life: To think clearly without hurry or confusion; To love everybody sincerely; To act in everything with the highest motives; To trust God unhesitatingly. Helen Keller
You can find my book: Indelible Indelibles at Amazon.com

Zielinski, Donald G.

Born and raised in Sudbury, Ontario, Canada, and now residing here. I have also lived in Milwaukee (Wisconsin), Montreal (province of Quebec). and Toronto,(province of Ontario). Je parle le Francais, aussi .and I also speak Friendshipian, Romancian, Loveian, and Lustian when it is appropriate :-)).....An A. P. member since July 5, 2014 :-))

Index
Of
Poets

Index

A.

B.

C.

D.

Davis, Carol (USA) 203
Daws, Chris (Chris the Rhymer) (United Kingdom) 113
Dayenoble (Canada) 42, 43
Donoghue, Susanne (Ecuador) 158, 198
Drikus 284

E.

Edwin, Kayanja Ronald (PoetR) 73
Emery, Alison (Deviantpixie) (USA) 129, 197, 237, 253, 271, 277
Emery, Allan (Joe King) (USA) 1, 136, 137, 192, 202, 207, 222, 236 Ezekiel, Ogbest (USA) 148

F.

Frost, Robert (USA) 117

G.

Gassingon (United Kingdom) 175, 289
Gee, Lulu (United Kingdom) 185, 249, 259, 290, 291, 299, 300, 301
Geiger, Paul (Pauljg) (USA) 29
Gilbert Eisenlord, Karen Lee (klge) (USA) 173
Gilchrist, Ann (Soulo) (Australia) 74, 75, 76, 226
Gogo, Carrie Mercedes 210
grandniem (USA) 78
Green, Sue K. (USA) 39, 41, 65
Grommett, Laurie F. (L.G.) (USA)19, 30, 72, 100, 110, 130, 150, 182, 214, 215, 247, 294, 295
Gupta, Arjita (India) 227

H.

Hamby Goss, Melody (Melody G) (USA) 70, 114, 204
Hartford, Dave (Anguish) (USA) 71

Lindemann, Cliff (Cuul) (South Africa) 54
Littleford, Norman (serious clown) (Great Britain) 10

M.

Matin, Sept (Sipeta) (Iran) 252, 258
McRight Jr., James W. (haikujourney) (USA)101
Moir, Mark (Great Britain) 102, 103, 168
Morkunaite, Emilija (USA) 66
Mosley, Ben (Perpatetic) (USA) 16, 17
Muir, Alistair (Al Muir) (England) 37, 120, 209
Mukherjee, Rajkumar (Rajkumar) (India) 56, 57, 191
Mullen, Jack (USA) 13, 146, 147, 164, 165, 166, 302, 303

N.

Nazeer, Dr. Asghar (United Arab Emirates) 40, 98, 99, 170, 171, 188, 194, 195, 200, 201
Nichols, James (Mindful) 50, 51

O.

Oday, Maria (Miz Rea) (USA) 48, 54, 133, 135, 150, 168
Owens, Andrea (USA) 122, 159. 175

P.

Paavolainen, V.S. (Finland) 104, 105, 106, 141, 142, 143, 144
Pappas, Chrysanthy (Arria1) (USA) 107, 108, 109, 134, 154, 162, 163, 176
Peake, Stephen (StephenPK) (USA) W. 44, 45, 88, 89
Petryshyn, Ivan (USA) 288
Pier, Kaleb (Iambthewalrus) (USA) 224, 225, 234, 235, 240, 244, 257
Pollard, Bev (witterwax) (New Zealand) 35, 86, 87

R.

Rangorth, Satheesan (Rangorth) (India) 7

Z.

Donors Index

Essama Chiba
James C. Allen
Dave Kavanagh
Diane Gwynne Allen
Ben Mosley
Paul Geiger
Vincent Donoghue
Anonymous
Francine Lentini
Anonymous
Mark Andrew James Terry
Susanne Donoghue
Katharine Sparrow
Shoestring Book Publishing
Rajkumar Mukherjee
Karen Eisenlord
Chrysanthy Pappas
Debra Joseph
Laurie F. Grommett
Benjamin Mosley
Jack Mullen
Deb Blondell Pitt

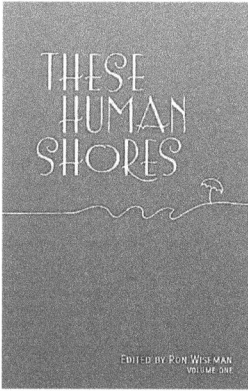

ISBN-13: 978-1490384153   **ISBN-13:** 978-1493755509

ISBN 13: 978-1500667672

Other Books Published By
The International Poetry Fellowship
Founded by Ron Wiseman
These Human Shores: Volumes 1, 2 & 3
Available in Paperback, Hardcover & ebook

Other Publications by Ron Wiseman:

Founder of the International Poetry Fellowship:

Prism 18, February 2016

ISBN13: 9781329917613

This book and previous volumes

can be found at Lulu.com

This book and previous Volumes

can be found at Lulu.com

Books by Michael Thomas avalable at Amazon

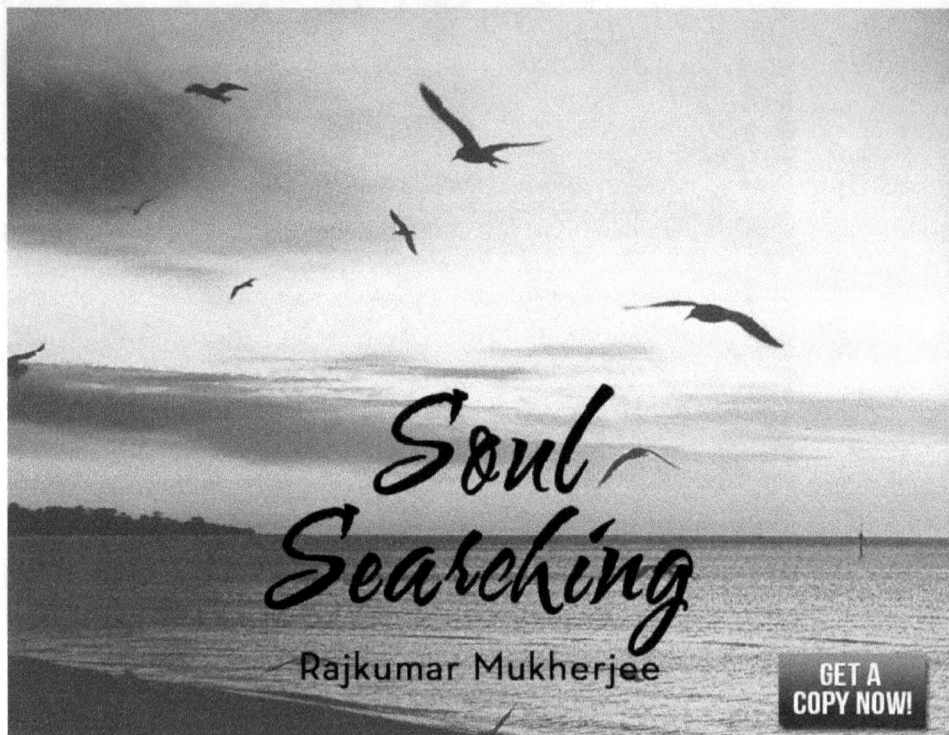

Soul Searching

Rajkumar Mukherjee

Published in September of 2016

Available in paperback on Amazon!

Saying Goodbye to Rue

James C. Allen

Available at Amazon!

Available at Amazon!

AVAILABLE AT AMAZON

Ink Angels, our second poetry book.

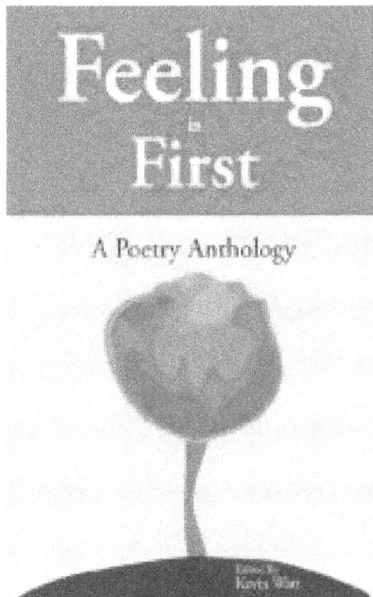

These and other fine books by independent authors
can be located at The Truthbrary Bookstore:
http://www.shoestringbookpublishing.com/truthbrary
bookstore.html

Shoestring Book Publishing offers simple
and affordable quality book publishing.

The smart choice
for the wise independent authors voice!

Send publishing inquiries to:
Shoestringpublishing4u@gmail.com

Visit: www.shoestringbookpublishing.com

IPF Members: receive 10% off any Publishing Services
listed at our website. (Excludes marketing packages.)

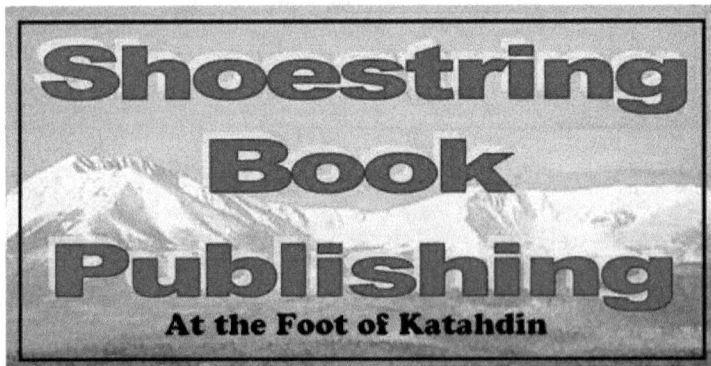

Shoestring Book Publishing
At the Foot of Katahdin

Please Review!

All independent authors depend upon reviews left on Amazon.com by readers to help promote their books. Without these reviews, they will hardly get any notice. Please take the time to leave a short review. Simply go to Amazon.com, find the book and go to the book's page. Under the author's name will be a list of reviews and stars. Click here and there will be a big button saying "Create your own review".

It only takes a minute!

www.ingramcontent.com/pod-product-compliance
Lightning Source LLC
Chambersburg PA
CBHW051936090426
42741CB00008B/1171